new
decoupage

Philadelphia
rococo silver

Napoleon and
Josephine's
Malmaison

Tiffany and the
Havemeyers

John Dwight,
London potter

Early travel
photographs

new

TRANSFORMING YOUR HOME WITH PAPER, GLUE, AND SCISSORS

decoupage

DURWIN RICE
PHOTOGRAPHS BY GEORGE ROSS

Clarkson Potter/Publishers
New York

Copyright © 1998 by Durwin Rice
Photographs copyright © 1998 by George Ross
Photograph page 21 used by permission of The Museum of
Modern Art; page 34 © 1998 by Bill Buckner; page 135 ©
Susan Johnson; page 136: top left, Sarah Feather; bottom
left, Katherine Simpson

Published by Clarkson N. Potter/Publishers
201 East 50th Street, New York, New York 10022.
Member of the Crown Publishing Group.

Random House, Inc. New York, Toronto,
London, Sydney, Auckland
www.randomhouse.com

CLARKSON N. POTTER, POTTER, and colophon are
trademarks of Clarkson N. Potter, Inc.

Manufactured in China

Design by Helene Silverman

Library of Congress Cataloging-in-Publication Data
Rice, Durwin.
    New decoupage/by Durwin Rice.
    1. Decoupage. I. Title.
TT870.R465   1998   97-45787
745.54'6–dc21   CIP
ISBN 0-517-70560-5
10   9   8   7   6   5   4   3   2   1
First Edition

ACKNOWLEDGMENTS

I NEVER used to read authors' acknowledgments. They were too much like Academy Award acceptance speeches, too many names that I thought meant nothing, except to the actor who didn't have the guts not to mention them all. Well, that was then, this is now. Now I am a big reader of an author's acknowledgments, because I understand that books just can't happen without the prodigious talents of people like Pam Krauss, Margot Schupf, George Ross, Lewis Bloom, Marysarah Quinn, Jane Treuhaft, and Helene Silverman. You'd be hard put to find a better team, so I suggest you call 'em up when you get ready to write your own.

Much of this book was accomplished at the Rectory of St. Paul's Memorial Church (Episcopal) in Staten Island, New York. This national landmark house was designed by Edward Tuckerman Potter in 1866, and it provided both a wonderful backdrop and a lot of subject material for New Decoupage. To St. Paul's Rector, Fr. William Blasingame, its parishioners, and also to the late Potter, I would like to say how blessed I was for the opportunity to work both in the house and with the parish family.

Finally, to my mother and sisters, who traveled the miles, rolled up their sleeves, and encouraged with their hearts, no "thank you" is ever going to be sufficient.

contents

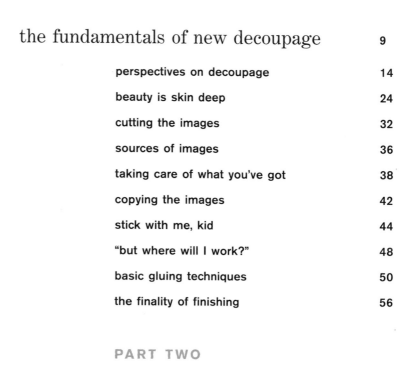

the fundamentals of new decoupage

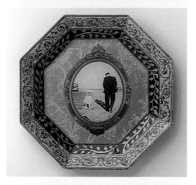

My first adventure in decoupage took place ten years ago. I was selling—or trying to sell—antiques. One day, while previewing an auction, I saw an old table, one made disreputable by what had befallen it: cigarette burns, discoloration, water-marks, stains. But beneath its scars, it bore the marks of good breeding. It was a rustic, sturdy, straightforward American piece. ✂ I bought it for a song, cleaned the surface, then lightly sanded and repainted it. The table looked better, but I wanted more. I knew about decoupage but had never tried it; here was my opportunity. ✂ I had been saving a roll of gorgeous old wallpaper that I'd found at a flea market in Kansas City. I decided to use sections of it to decorate the surface of the table. I didn't do anything too fussy, just a floral motif at each corner and a decorative center medallion. Not having a clue about what I was doing, I glued the paper on and gave the table two coats of polyurethane for protection. Two weeks later I sold the table to a gift shop for a lot more money than I had ever made selling any antique. ✂ But something else had happened, something that went beyond a good profit. I had enjoyed decoupaging the table. I had enjoyed transforming the plain, humdrum piece into something lively and attractive, and I had done it using simple techniques. ✂ In the first part of this book I detail those techniques in addition to sharing the many tricks

that I have learned over the last ten years. If you follow my advice and instructions, you shouldn't have any problems. But try not to get caught up in the if-it's-written-it-must-be-the-only-way fallacy. Experiment. Teach yourself. Mastery of any skill isn't mimicry; it's allowing your own creativity to enter into the picture. Most of all, have some fun.

perspectives on decoupage: A NEW TAKE ON AN OLD CRAFT

The Old Decoupage

"We are here in the height of a new passion for cutting up colored engravings. . . . Every lady, great and small, is cutting away. These cuttings are pasted on sheets of pasteboard and then varnished. We make wall panels, screens and fire boards of them. There are books and engravings that cost up to 100 lire apiece. If this fashion continues, they will cut up Raphaels."

Or so Madame Aïssé, an 18th-century Frenchwoman, noted in a letter to her sister. Decoupage had become popular in the century before Madame Aïssé's friends were eyeing the works of Raphael, who, aside from being Europe's favorite painter at the time, was also from Italy, the birthplace of decoupage. Some of the best examples of early decoupage are from Venice, and their creation was the result of a tangle of artistic and economic forces.

In the late 17th century, Venetian furniture was a hot export item; all of Europe was crazy for the stuff. The rage went beyond an appreciation for fine cabinet-making. Many Venetian artists would sketch lovely drawings on the furniture and then color them, creating a stunning combination of painting and furniture. Demand soon outpaced supply, and enterprising artists had thousands of their drawings printed. Then, instead of individually painting each piece of furniture, they'd sell the prints to cabinet-makers who glued them onto the furniture. Some modestly talented painter would fill in the colors—a Venetian version of painting by numbers. This was early decoupage, what some artists of the time called *l'arte del povero*, or poor man's art. Poor man's art or not, the furniture-makers laughed all the way to the Venetian banks.

Decoupage continued to be such a rage that valuable paintings by such noted artists as Fragonard, Boucher, and Watteau soon were being cut up and glued onto objects. Without all this snip, snip, snipping, art museums around the world might have even larger collec-

tions of 18th-century French paintings than they do now. In England one practitioner, Mary Delaney, managed to cut and paste on an almost microscopic level. Her work is unbelievably minute and endlessly fascinating. But the reign of decoupage would not last forever. In France, it went out with the ancien régime and, in fact, few French have practiced decoupage in the past 200 years.

By the middle of this century, decoupage had become an avocation of only a handful of devotees, most of them mired in the floral-draped cherub fantasies of the late 19th century. I'm thankful they kept up the tradition but bored to death by their fussiness. They made decoupage a genteel avocation as restrictive as a whalebone corset and focused on little things—plates, boxes, lampshades, and trays. This approach may still work for some people, but I think it's time for a change.

New Decoupage

The time has come to bring the art of decoupage out of the closet of fussy delicacy and take a fresh look at an old craft. This new take might encompass motifs and styles that have influenced Western civilization, including baroque, rococo, Victorian, and even modern, to name a few. But I don't like to apply such rigid stylistic classifications to decoupage works. For people interested in transforming some decorative element in their environment, such classifications can be stultifying. An overemphasis upon a particular style or period can limit creativity, confining a decoupeur (that is, one who practices decoupage) to approaches that are wedded to the wandering lines of the rococo, the impeccable balance of the classical age, or even the bizarre asymmetries of our own time. That would be unfortunate, because decoupage is not the exclusive property of any age or school of design.

I propose New Decoupage—a decoupage that's not just about pasting sweet paper flowers onto Victorian saucers. Rather, New Decoupage is about incorporating images into other things. The images are usually (but not always) paper, and the manipulation may take one or more forms. Thanks to the laser photocopier, images can be reformatted by being resized. Or, by cutting and combining them with other images, they may be understood in a new context. Finally, the images are manipulated by the decoupeur by being applied to a surface. The surface could be that of a Victorian saucer, but practitioners of New Decoupage don't limit their thinking. Why call yourself creative and then go about setting limits on what you can and can't do? Saucers are fine, but so is every other surface in the universe. I love flowers and gardens, but if a series of camels decoupaged around the frame of my bathroom mirror gives me a little lift in the morning, why shouldn't I find me some camels?

New Decoupage is also about transformation. Through it you can transform a trinket into an objet d'art, a disreputable table into a decorating focal point, or a nondescript ceiling into an architectural treasure. It's about images that you like, from the exotic to the mundane and everything in between. New Decoupage can be as surreal as it is real; it can be as straitlaced as a Victorian tea party or as unbridled as an expensive night in a cheap hotel.

Understand this: To be a great decoupeur (yes, you can be great) you don't have to be another Michelangelo. Who can? But thanks to modern publishing and photocopying, you can *create* like Michelangelo, appropriating his images for your own use.

Take the Sistine Chapel ceiling. I did.

Yes, I know some purists will protest that Michelangelo's work is a great theological assertion that is most appropriate on the ceiling of the chamber where the College of Cardinals selects a new pope.

Well, it *is* a great theological assertion, one that touches me deeply.

OPPOSITE: *Yes, this really is my kitchen ceiling. You may go nuts if you decide to do this at home and then try to match up every little corner. My advice is, don't. Just overlap the edges and don't get upset if you dislocate Adam's elbow from his wrist. If you obsess on all the tiny things that go wrong, you'll never get to the finish line.*

So why shouldn't it hang over me as I make dinner every night?

Up until a few years ago, such a ceiling would have been merely a pipe dream. The Sistine Chapel ceiling couldn't have hung above me unless I found a great Michelangelo forger who would willingly paint my kitchen ceiling in return for a spaghetti dinner. Today, however—thanks to companies like Xerox, Kodak, and Canon—I don't have to worry about finding a hungry forger. All I need is a good color picture of the Sistine Chapel ceiling (from an art history book, for example) and a color laser copier that can enlarge images—the kind found in many business offices and local copy shops. I take my picture (in this case, *The Creation of Man*) and make an enlarged version to occupy a central position on my kitchen ceiling. Then, armed with the relatively simple skills of a decoupeur, I glue the paper to the ceiling, polyurethane it, and voilà! a miniature Sistine Chapel.

If the work of Michelangelo doesn't appeal to you, how about a color photograph of the vaulting in a medieval cathedral? Such photographs abound in books on architecture. Photocopy the central rib, the groins, the tiercerones, the whatevers, then enlarge them to fit the dimensions of your room. Within a few minutes you'll have the

RIGHT: *You don't have to be a multimillionaire to have a pretty punch bowl like this . . . just laser copy a priceless Fabergé design, cut, glue, finish, et voilà!*

raw materials of a Gothic ceiling in your hands, but, instead of being as heavy as stone, they'll be as light as paper. Once assembled, the effect can be mesmerizing.

Or just have some fun. A glass plate can have a portrait of J. S. Bach on one side and Tina Turner on the other, and you don't have to explain why, because it's your plate, your choice, your interpretation. With a few basic materials and your own creativity, you have all you need to create incredible, imaginative works of decoupage art.

Don't let the word *creativity* spook you. Being creative, being artistic, even being an artist, doesn't mean you need the talent of Michelangelo, just the willingness to transform your environment without heed to any "established" artistic standards but your own.

I learned this lesson a long time ago, in a sun-filled third-grade classroom just outside Kansas City, Missouri. Our art teacher, Mrs. Shine, terrified me that day by her instructions, "Now, children, I want you to paint a picture depicting some shadows."

I had been sitting in her class for twenty minutes and these were the first words of hers that I had actually heard. They certainly weren't her first words; she'd been talking all that time and even demonstrating with watercolors how to achieve various shadow effects. But I had been daydreaming. Now I didn't have a clue what to do. So I gazed off into space again, hoping some revelation would come to me.

One did.

LEFT: *The Tricycle Project. A work in progress by the Pre-School Children's Art Studio Classes in the Art Lab at Snug Harbor, Staten Island. There's no end to what these kids can come up with to paste onto this tricycle. Which brings us to one of the big questions: how do you know when it's a good time to stop adding to your own decoupage creations? Look, these kids are just having some fun. There's your answer.*

With only a few minutes left in class, I picked up my scissors and cut two diagonal sides of a triangle into a blank sheet of white paper. I bent the cut piece out toward me, held it up to the light, and prayed that the protruding paper would create the longed-for shadow. It did. I painted some green pine trees onto the protruding paper and finished the piece off as a mountain slope with a couple of skiers. I handed in my creation.

The next day Mrs. Shine entered the classroom with all the projects under her left arm. Mine was on top. She held it up. "Class, we have something here that's very good. I asked you to paint a shadow. But Durwin has actually created a shadow. Durwin is *creative*."

I shyly accepted the honor and learned a valuable lesson. You don't have to be a genius to make something wonderful. You just have to want to do it and be willing to try.

Decoupage . . . What Is It, Anyway?

Ask most people to explain decoupage, and dollars to doughnuts they'll talk about flowers and cherubs in a Victorian-style collage. Yes, that is a *style* of decoupage, but it isn't the very definition of decoupage. The more informed might tell you it's about cutting and pasting; that's better, but while cutting and pasting are important, they comprise only some of the techniques of decoupage, not the art of decoupage. The art of decoupage is in the reformatting of paper onto (or perhaps into) something else. Decoupeurs find their source materials almost anyplace: magazines, art books, auction catalogues, photographs, junk mail, newspapers, that pile of letters under the bed—you name it—and then reformat them onto another surface—a box, a plate, a canvas, furniture, mirrors, frames, walls, floors, ceilings, themselves. In short, what paint is to painting, and what words are to literature, paper and paper images are to decoupage.

Consider Matisse, late in his career, sitting amid scattered bits of paper in his studio, assiduously cutting. Matisse used paper cut-outs as a creative medium, a tool to express his vision as an artist. After all, an artist's work does re-examine the way we look at the world (or at ourselves), which is also what New Decoupage allows you to do. But New Decoupage is uninhibited artistry. No one calls decoupeurs geniuses (even though some, like Matisse, clearly were), and that's good, because it would scare away too many people who might otherwise enjoy and benefit from this craft.

I can't stress this enough: New Decoupage is about transforming your environment—whether it's a dull refrigerator, a child's tired room, a lackluster dining room, or a boring piece of furniture.

After college, I moved to New York City from the Midwest. I came for the opportunity to make a life that I wanted. Big cities like New York offer people the chance to become who they want to be, free to

realize their potential, free to sing a new song. Big cities don't lock you in, and neither does New Decoupage.

New Decoupage is an old art form that has been revitalized in the hands of contemporary men and women who want to remake a part of their world and give that part their personal stamp. New Decoupage doesn't tell you what to do; you tell it what to do. You're the boss. You're the artist.

To transform an environment, most people think they need pots of money. After all, how can you change a bare-walled livingroom in a Brooklyn apartment into an English clubroom? But on this point most people are wrong. New Decoupage allows you to transform a space with nothing more than paper images, sharp scissors, adhesive, sealant, and a willingness to be led by your creative instincts.

Try it. Lift a Monet water lily from a magazine page. Borrow a border from a piece of wallpaper. Filch a photograph from a cookbook. Snatch a car from a newspaper ad. These images are your raw materials; you are the artist controlling them.

I'll say it again—you can decoupage just about anything. You only need to invest a little time and energy in learning to do the job right.

BELOW: *The artist at home (Kansas City, 1958). Dreaming of one day joining the campaign to elect Richard Nixon to president of the United States.*

OPPOSITE: *These snazzy bookends are decoupage under glass that has been mounted to wood. Their combined weight does a nifty job at holding my Nixon collection together.*

beauty
is skin
deep: PROPER PREPARATION

The rule is simple. In order to end up with a smooth finished product you must begin with an undecorated surface that is both clean and smooth, as in *very clean* and *very smooth*. A properly prepared surface is the best way to ensure that your project turns out the way you want it to. Any imperfections in the surface will show up in your final product. Though minor blemishes might not totally ruin your creation, a few simple steps can prevent them.

So how do you get things so clean and smooth? First, consider the properties of the surface. Is it wood? If so, is it finished, unfinished, painted, or varnished? Is it new or old, oily or waxed? Are you planning to decoupage onto metal, plastic, plaster, or foam core? I could come up with countless surfaces and even more surface conditions that you might encounter in your decoupage career, so how does one learn to properly prepare each and every one? Experience. I'll begin with the most common and frequently used surfaces for decoupage. What follows are the best ways to clean and prepare each and some ideas on how to attack surfaces that present unique challenges.

Cleaning the Surface

GLASS. If the surface you're working on is glass, use soap and water to clean it. If you've still got streaks, switch to any of the glass cleaners found on supermarket shelves. I know what you're thinking: I didn't have to buy this book to find that out. And you certainly didn't have to buy this book to find out that, if the glass is painted, you can carefully remove unwanted paint with a single-edge razor blade. It won't scratch the surface as long as you hold the blade flat against the glass.

WOOD. If you're working on new and untreated wood, fresh out of the lumberyard, it should already be clean or you shouldn't have bought it. Same goes for unfinished wood products and furniture that's already assembled.

However, if the wood surface is old and has been waxed, oiled, or painted, things get more complicated. Of all of these challenges, a painted surface is generally the easiest to deal with, so let's begin with painted surfaces.

Your course of action depends, naturally, on the finished product you desire. If you like the condition of the paint—distressed, pristine, or something in between—and if you like the color as a background for your project simply wash the surface thoroughly with household soap and water. On the other hand, if you hate the color, use a medium- to fine-grit sandpaper to sand the entire surface until it's flat and without luster. This will ensure that the new paint you're

BELOW: *Old serving trays, the kind found at flea markets, may be junk to most people, but they are just ripe for decoupage decoration. Don't worry if they're worn, corroded, and disgusting. Sand them down and decoupage them to death.*

going to apply will stick. Once you are done sanding, wipe the surface with a damp cloth. Let the surface dry and then paint away. Two coats of latex paint will usually suffice as a basecoat, provided you haven't bought really cheap paint. Believe me, there are valid reasons that some companies charge more for their products.

If the paint is old, ugly, and peeling, and you're not into that distressed look, then you've got to strip away all the old paint. A variety of products can do this. Seek advice from the staff at your local hardware store and *be sure to read the label* for application instructions suitable for each product.

But why not consider using the distressed paint as a background? I've seen some lovely decoupage projects that simply skipped the stripping step and used the distressed paint finish to very good advantage. All you need to do is sand lightly, to remove flaking or peeling paint, and then seal the surface with two coats of acrylic polyurethane before applying your images. But do this only if you want the finished piece to have an antique look, in which case unevenness in the surface becomes an asset.

If the wood you're eyeing has been waxed or oiled, the wax or oil must be removed completely before you apply anything (be it paint, stain, sealer, or adhesive). Otherwise whatever you apply will end up doing an imitation of a bad sunburn—peel, peel, peel.

To avoid peeling, thoroughly clean the oily or waxed wood surface with mineral spirits, available at any hardware or craft supply store. If the surface feels at all tacky, wax or oil is still present; repeat the application of mineral spirits. If you doubt the piece will ever be clean, take a closer look at it. Maybe you've discovered a Jacobean chest from the 17th century that isn't going to benefit at all from your decoupage intentions, or maybe the chest is just beyond rescuing. So don't ruin a great piece of furniture and, just as important, don't ruin your life trying to rescue a piece of junk.

METAL. Fortunately you'll have no such problems with metal. Metal is impermeable. It does not drink in oil or wax; therefore, it is usually easy to clean. Just wipe it down thoroughly with soap and warm water, and and dry it thoroughly before you begin. If the old metal tray you picked up at a garage sale is painted, use coarse sandpaper to remove any loose paint. Then rub the rest with steel wool. On the other hand, if the tray has some nicely painted flowers or fruits, you may want to forego sanding in those areas and consider incorporating the existing design into your creation.

All traces of rust, however, must be removed. Rust is extremely sneaky. That beautiful old tray you found at the flea market with just a bit of rust on the corner may turn out to be mostly rust beneath the paint. You must meticulously sand away the paint and then sand away the rust. After you're completely satisfied that the rust has been vanquished, apply a coat of rust-inhibiting primer to the exposed metal.

PLASTIC. Plastic surfaces represent no unique challenges. Make sure they are clean and smooth; this can be achieved by using a fine-grit sandpaper and/or a regular household spray cleaner. Just don't hurry the drying process by using a hair dryer after you've finished your decoupage masterpiece. I was late on a consignment order once, and you guessed it, the tray began to melt.

If you're not sure about what to use to clean a specific surface, ask an expert. It doesn't have to be the chairman of the local college chemistry department. Go to a local hardware store. People who own hardware stores know more about surface preparation than anyone else. In fact, they seem to know more about everything than anyone else, with the possible exception of hairstylists. Whether it's a midlife crisis, social alienation, or correct surface preparation, ask your local hardware store owner.

IMCOMPATIBLE PROCEDURES

An obvious but often unspoken household rule is this: don't make meringues where you change the oil in the car; certain procedures don't mix. Sanding and gluing are two of them. So are sanding and sealing. Nothing wrecks an adhesive or polyurethane coat more effectively than minute particles from sanding. Sand in the basement, outside, in your garage, in your bed, sand anywhere you want, but *don't sand where you glue or where you seal.*

Smoothing the Surface

In addition to being clean, you may decide that you want to restore a slightly uneven surface to its original pristine smoothness, because it doesn't take a lot of thought to realize that imperfections—lumps, depressions, ridges—will show through your completed work, especially if you finish the project with a high-gloss sealant. However, if it's not possible to remove every irregularity, don't despair. Just make sure to use a matte-sheen product to finish your work. Matte finishes minimize imperfections; high-gloss finishes tend to maximize them.

There are two easy ways of smoothing an uneven surface. One is to sand the surface down. The other is to fill it in. As a general rule, you should sand if most of the surface is already smooth except for a few modest elevations. Fill in the surface if it is smooth except for a few modest depressions.

SANDING. If smoothing the surface of an old piece, begin with fairly coarse sandpaper. Press hard enough to remove imperfections but don't exhaust your arms. Switch to a coarser paper, if necessary, or to a less coarse paper if you judge you're doing more damage than good. How much you sand and the paper you use depends on how smooth you want the finished surface to be. Sandpapers are graded from coarse to medium to very, very fine. The higher the grade number, the finer the grit. Once you get above Grade 200, you are in the fine category.

On new wood, begin with medium-grit paper, say Grade 80 or 100. Gradually advance to fine-grit paper and sand until you achieve the smoothness you want. Rest when your arm gets tired. Investment in a handheld electric sander is a good idea if you're planning to do a lot of sanding, but it's certainly not necessary for most small projects.

When you're done sanding, wipe the surface with a damp rag or sponge to remove dust particles. Don't get the wood wet, or it might swell. An alternative to wiping is using a vacuum cleaner, provided you can find the brush attachment. Use a tack cloth if you insist on obsessing about the microscopic bits.

FILLING. If the surface is smooth except for a few depressions or holes, you'll want to fill them in. Ready-mixed plasters, plaster of paris, plastic woods, and gessoes are easy to use. Follow the manufacturer's instructions and, after filling in the depressions, allow the filler to dry thoroughly. Sand the area lightly until it's even with the surrounding surface. Each product and each brand is different, so check the label to find the correct drying time and the correct grades of sandpaper to use.

OPPOSITE: *Notice the symmetrical arrangement of violins on this tray table. Symmetry suggests order, and order is a good thing. So maybe its time for you to clean up your room?*

Sealing the Surface

If you're working on wood, make up your mind before you begin: Do you want a painted or stained background? If you've decided to go for a painted background on raw wood, you need to seal the surface with a paint primer. Following the instructions on the can, prime the surface with two coats; allow each coat to dry thoroughly. You are now ready to paint.

If it's a stained wood background you want, first choose the color of stain you like. Once again, the best instructions will be on the can of whatever stain you've chosen. In one sense, staining wood is the same as staining clothing. The longer you leave the stain on the wood, the darker the stain will become. So apply wood stain with a bristle brush and wipe it off immediately with an absorbent rag. If the result is too light in color, you can always repeat the application to achieve a darker result. After the requisite drying time (check the label), seal the stained surface with two coats of acrylic polyurethane. What's that you've found on the hardware store shelf? An oil-based polyurethane? It's true that an oil-based polyurethane will give you a somewhat smoother surface, but the fumes will mess with your brain unless you use the product in a well-ventilated space. If you use an oil-based polyurethane, follow label instructions carefully. Most of the time an acrylic polyurethane will suffice. I recommend oil-based products for only those projects whose surface must be supersmooth.

One Last Point about Surface Preparation Before We Move on to the Fun Stuff

Suppose the surface is more than slightly irregular. Say it's more like the forehead of a hormone-ridden, chocolate-eating teenager—bumpy, uneven, pitted, and splintery. Weigh the amount of time you will spend smoothing it down against the overall value of the piece. You may conclude that it's a waste of time, or you may conclude that bumpy, uneven, pitted, and splintery is good. After all, where is it written that a distressed surface is always bad? Okay, it's bad on a 15-year-old, but on an object intended to spice up your living space, it can add an interesting texture and antique quality.

OPPOSITE: *I spotted this door one day on a street in Staten Island and put it in the back of my pickup. Months later I met an artist who had moved here from Denver. One day she visited my house and told me she had brought that same door with her from Colorado—she'd kept it for about a year, before finally abandoning her idea of working with it. We all just love it, but nobody knows what to do with it. Anybody got any ideas?*

cutting the images: SOME RAZOR-SHARP ADVICE

Cutting is to decoupage what brushwork is to a painting; it's part of the craft, a skill in and of itself. Cutting will be easier if you give some attention to paper types, cutting tools, and technique.

Paper Types: What You Cut Makes a Difference

There is unanimous consensus among the cutters in my studio: The easiest paper to cut is the paper that comes out of the laser copier. At the other end of the spectrum, among the most challenging papers to cut well is magazine paper, such as the glossy stock *Time* magazine is printed on. That paper tends to be flimsy and rips easily. This is unfortunate because it is on magazine stock that you frequently find the diversity of images you need, red-hot photographs of Madonna right next to the Pope. The best solution to this dilemma is to photocopy the magazine image and then cut the reproduction. That way, you have the image on paper that is easy to cut.

Another solution is to forget about sources like *Time*. Expand your horizons. There are tons of really gorgeous images each month in full-color art magazines such as *Art & Antiques* and *Architectural Digest*, and the weight of their paper is a bit heavier than that in general-interest magazines and consequently easier to cut. And then there are art books and auction catalogues. These have wonderful images and are generally printed on high-quality paper.

Cutting Tools

A lot has been written on the subject of cutting tools. Some of it is very misleading. Take cuticle scissors, for instance. Take them and throw them out—unless you're a manicurist.

Why cut with hard-to-grasp little cuticle scissors? And beware of those shrink-wrapped scissors in crafts stores advertised as decoupage scissors. They're part of the equipment emphasis of our

OPPOSITE: *An Olfa knife is a great tool to have in your decoupage arsenal. When the blade gets dull, you just snap it off and you are left with a fresh, sharp blade. The green surface that we are working on is a self-healing mat. Don't try and figure out how you can cut into this mat without actually cutting it, just get yourself one.*

time, which maintains that you can't jog, play tennis, or hit a golf ball unless you do so with the best equipment (which usually happens to be the most expensive equipment). I don't buy that, and neither should you, at least when it comes to purchasing cutting tools.

All you need to begin is a sharp pair of scissors that feel comfortable in your hand and maybe an Olfa or X-acto knife, which is merely a small razor blade inserted into something that resembles a pen. This knife will help with the finest of fine details, and is available at an art supply or well-stocked hardware stores.

For nearly every cutting situation, I prefer an inexpensive—but sharp—pair of Fiskars scissors. I have a big hand, and for me the

Fiskars are comfortable. And because the blade is long, I can cut a lot farther and faster than I can with cuticle scissors. In my studio, my chief cutter prefers 8-inch scissors from her sewing basket. The point is, use whatever feels best to you.

Cutting Techniques

• Discussion of technique is useless if not prefaced by the command to keep your scissors *sharp*. If your scissors won't cut through a piece of damp construction paper easily, they're dull. Get a new pair or have them professionally sharpened—say, at a hardware store.

• The fewer times you open and close your blades, the better. Most people think the best way to cut is snip, snip, snip; that's wrong, wrong, wrong. The right way is to feed, feed, feed. Whether it's a straight line you want or a circle, feed your paper into the blade, moving the hand holding the scissors as little as possible. The result will be fewer, or possibly even no, jagged edges. Trust me.

• Don't be obsessive. Fanatical cutting is for, well, fanatics. You are master of the image, not the image of you.

• Be flexible. If the image of the pink rose you love is too large for your intended surface, make it fit. Cut off a couple of petals. It's not a mortal sin. It's creativity.

• And speaking of flowers, remember that stems are not sacred. Cut through the stem if it gets in your way; you can easily graft it back together during the gluing process. In fact, an elaborate image *ought* to be broken down into small parts, which will be easier to glue than one big image. Why make things difficult?

• Don't be afraid to cut into the image, at least a little bit. It's better to trim off a bit of the image than it is to leave the unsightly line of an obtrusive background clinging to the edges.

One last thing to consider about cutting: You don't always have to. Some images are available precut and perfectly sized. You can use Post-it® notes (ideal for making geometric designs), stamps, postcards, or labels instead of cutting paper into pieces of similar size. You can also "cut" by using your fingers. I often rip handmade papers to create uneven and interesting borders. If you want your serving tray to mimic the frenetic, nervous energy that your mother-in-law has perfected, then a ragged edge might be just the thing.

OPPOSITE: *My favorite dog, my favorite papers . . . God's in his heaven.*

sources of images: BECOMING AN IMAGE PACK RAT

TAKING CHARGE OF YOUR CREATIVITY

Collecting images needn't be a last-minute ordeal, something you do only after you've decided to decoupage an object. Make artwork collecting an ongoing process, even a hobby. If you see a great image, cut it out—even if you don't have plans for it. Something will pop up. With a wonderful collection of images on hand, you'll have constant inspiration for endless projects.

The best images on the best paper are usually in art books. Am I suggesting you go a museum shop or bookstore and plunk down $50 for a book so you can cut it up? Well, yes, if you like wasting money. If you like bargains, consider this: Find secondhand art books at flea markets and rummage sales. They may be shopworn, but usually only the outside is damaged. Inside you will find a treasure trove of great images.

Get to know the volunteers at thrift shops. Let them know what you are looking for. Most will be glad to call you when something you want arrives.

Don't overlook any source of photos or illustrations. Toy catalogues, anatomy books, cookbooks, postcard collections, outdated calendars—all could contain images that might work for you. And, since we're being shamelessly frugal, don't forget to look in other people's trash. It's amazing what wonderful stuff gets thrown out.

Next, you should save your pennies, plan a trip to New York City, and pay about $25 for a guest pass to the National Stationery Show. You'll find the wares of a gazillion companies that make or import handmade papers, wrapping papers, greeting cards, art books, calendars, date books, stationery, and all manner of things printed.

Your local auction house, no matter how seedy it may look from the outside, is a trove of decoupage images as well as things to decoupage. Stop in during a preview and see what is hidden in the boxed lots.

And don't think only in terms of books for your images. An old scrap of fabric can laser-copy beautifully. A Patsy Cline album cover might make a great border for your next decoupage tray.

Friends and family are terrific resources as well. Remember those napkins that didn't quite match Aunt Mary's tablecloth? How about Uncle Waldo's obscene playing cards that Aunt Mary will not have in the house? Consider that extra roll of wallpaper that your sister's first husband insisted they were going to need and the date book cousin Beatrice will never, ever use. All are potential image sources.

Libraries, however, are off limits. The British playwright Joe Orton once wound up in jail for pilfering images from the local library and decoupaging them onto his bedroom wall. Even if you're a great playwright, robbing the local library is not a nice thing to do.

In short, just about anything printed is at your disposal, as well as anything that the local copy shop will let you put through the laser copier. In fact, if you want to, cut up this book. Just buy another one.

BELOW: *Big, flat drawers are ideal for storing images you've already cut. They keep out dust, pollen, children's hands, bathroom leaks, and nosy neighbors.*

taking care of what you've got: 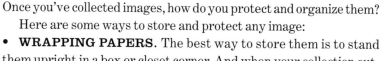STORAGE IDEAS

Once you've collected images, how do you protect and organize them? Here are some ways to store and protect any image:

- **WRAPPING PAPERS**. The best way to store them is to stand them upright in a box or closet corner. And when your collection outgrows your box (or closet) get a cardboard letter organizer from an office supply store and lay it on its backside with the openings facing up. The slots originally designed for memos are just the right size to hold your wrapping paper rolls.

- **FOLDED CONSTRUCTION-PAPER FILES**. Purchase 18- by 24-inch sheets of construction paper. Fold the 24-inch length once, and you've created a folder measuring 12 by 18 inches, an ideal place for storing 11- by 17-inch laser copies. These files also help to keep cut-up artwork flat and accessible, and they are excellent for storing pages and images from oversized art books and magazines.

- **8½- BY 11-INCH FILE FOLDERS**. These will hold pages from auction catalogues and most magazines.

- **ENVELOPES**. Standard business envelopes can keep your tiniest bits and pieces organized. For quick reference, be sure to write on the envelope what's inside. If your handwriting's not legible, even to you, paste or tape a sample of what's inside on the outside of the envelope.

- **PLASTIC BINS**. Flat plastic storage bins hold a lot of cut-up artwork, and you can stack them to save storage space. Label the top edge of each: "Yellow butterflies," "Antique toys," "Chinese take-out menus," "Celebrities I hate," etc. Label one tray "To be filed"—inevitably you will find bits around your work space that need to be put away, and it's best to place them into this bin until you can find the

ABOVE: *When you find unique images that you fall in love with but don't know what to do with, tape or tack them onto the wall in your work space. The repeated exposure to the image will eventually give you a great idea.*

time to do your filing. If you're like me and hate to file, create a decoupage masterpiece with all these unfiled images. Title it *To Be Filed* and sell it for a lot of money. It worked for me.

- **IN A BOOK**. Very delicate pieces of cut paper are best kept separate, laid flat and tucked inside the pages of a heavy book. Be sure to label the spine so you can find the images when you need them.

- **THROW IT OUT**. It's also important not to over-obsess when you are collecting and organizing. The decoupeur who can (occasionally) edit his collection will get a lot further, creatively speaking.

BELOW: *Besides collecting images, why not pick up a clear glass or crystal vase if you see one you like? That way you'll always have something on hand to decoupage.*

copying the images: CLONING YOUR COLLECTION

As I mentioned earlier, one of the greatest allies of New Decoupage is the color laser copier. It not only duplicates, it makes images bigger or smaller, wider or longer. It intensifies colors and can even "antique" an image by giving it a sepia tint. Plus, for those of us who find ordinary rulers to be complicated machines, it is remarkably easy to use.

You can find a color laser copier in almost any local copy shop. If you're gun-shy about using it yourself, don't worry; the owner, who paid an arm and a leg for it, probably won't let you use it yourself anyway. You'll be put into the hands of the presumably capable attendant. Tell him or her how many copies you want, what colors you'd like intensified or muted, and whether you want the image enlarged or shrunk. If the attendant doesn't understand what you're talking about, ask for the machine's instruction manual and a chair. Sit down, order a pizza, and find out what you need to know. Then, you tell the attendant what to do.

For me, the most exciting aspect about working with a laser copier is its ability to enlarge or reduce images. By simply setting the x and y coordinates (the horizontal and the vertical) to a particular size, you can manipulate an image to fit almost any space. For example, it was the ability to enlarge an image of a pot of flowers to the exact specifications of my cabinets that helped me to create a lovely kitchen interior (see page 124). The same ability allowed me to shrink my Aunt Flo's hips on an image I decoupaged to a plate, thereby pleasing Aunt Flo and securing my place in her will.

You can also make images significantly larger than you might think by laser-copying different sections of an image onto different pieces of paper. All you have to do is fit them together and glue them into place. That is how the 10- by 16-inch image of the pot of flowers became 2½ by 3 feet.

Another amazing thing the laser copier can do is make mirror im-

42

ages. These are wonderful in creating elaborate designs, such as those you might want to put on the opposite sides of your decoupage bookends.

One last thing about color laser copiers: the Tranquil Color button. It's a good button to know about, considering that all laser photocopy machines aspire to be art directors. They adjust your colors without even asking you! Sometimes that's just ducky; other times, it's a pain in the neck. If you're copying an image that happens to be faded, the copier will automatically try to goose up the colors. But what if you like those faded tones? You certainly don't want HAL, the laser copier, turning them into bright neons. Luckily, you can program the copier to leave your preferred colors alone by pressing the Tranquil Color button. This tells the copier to back off and copy what it sees, not what it thinks it should see.

Don't think for a moment that's all there is to know about color laser copiers. But that's all I needed to know to produce most of the art in this book. But since technology marches on faster than most of us can run, make it a point to ask lots of questions when you're in the copy shop. Call the hotlines at Canon, Kodak, and Xerox and ask for advice if you're working on your own. Find out which copy shops in your area have the newest equipment and which attendants know the most about the equipment they're using.

stick with me, kid:

THE ZANY WORLD OF ADHESIVES

All right. You've properly prepared the surface, neatly cut the images, and thought about composition. Now you're ready to glue.

Not so fast. Before you glue, you need to take a side trip into the wonderful world of adhesives. Always keep this axiom in mind when thinking about glues: Your choice of adhesive and the amount to use will vary, depending on the paper and surface you're working with.

Different papers react very differently to the gluing process. I've lost plenty of beautiful images because I applied too little (or too much) glue when adhering a thin paper to a surface. If a mistake happens—and it will—I have only one thing to say: Laugh. You're not working with marble, where one slip can ruin the sculpture. You're working with paper and, if you mess up, you can always cut out another piece. So relax. New Decoupage is not as scary as that tenured professor who taught your freshman English class. It's fun.

The best way to learn about adhesives is to experiment. There are literally hundreds of types and brands, and they're all going to behave differently, depending on the paper, the surface you're working with, the humidity, and the temperature, even naughty suspicions you might have about your friends or family. If you doubt a suspicious nature can affect decoupage, I would point out that one gluer in my studio disintegrated a beautiful image of a rose because, she said, her fingers naturally crushed it after it reminded her of a rose her unfaithful and subsequently ex-husband had given her.

However, since you probably did not purchase this book to be told to experiment with glue (although I advise you to do so), I'll give you my hit parade of favorite glues and in what situations I think they work best.

Polyvinyl Acetates

Known by the abbreviation PVA, polyvinyl acetates are also called white glues because, you guessed it, they're white. A PVA was probably the glue that was in your paste pot back in kindergarten. The neat thing about a PVA is that, although it's white, it dries clear. This is the best adhesive for you to use with glass.

Some PVA can be toxic, however. So, if you think you or anybody near you will be tempted to taste the stuff, check the label for toxicity and purchase a PVA that is marked "nontoxic." My PVA of choice is nontoxic Elmer's Glue-All.

Wheat Paste and Wallpaper Pastes

This group of adhesives can be purchased ready-to-mix or ready-mixed. In terms of ease of use, wheat paste and wallpaper paste are the best adhesives available. There is less drag between the glued image and the surface, so images are less likely to tear and wrinkle. But although easy to work with, these adhesives are not nearly as strong an adhesive as PVA. So, if your project will have some practical use—a serving tray, for instance—use a PVA. If the work is just going to sit around and get admired for the rest of its life, then use wheat paste or wallpaper paste.

My Own Special Blend

Torn between the strong bond of a PVA and the workability of a wheat or wallpaper paste, I've worked out a compromise. By mixing approximately equal amounts of PVA with either paste, I've been able to create an adhesive that is both strong and workable. And it is a rare occasion when my mixture doesn't fit the bill.

On those rare occasions I create a custom blend of PVA and paste that is formulated to meet the need. How much of each ingredient to use? Put away your measuring cups and think of how your great-grandmother used to make bread. You never saw her measure a thing and hers is still the best bread you ever tasted. Just remember this rule: PVAs are strong and wheat and wallpaper pastes are weak, so use a greater amount of PVA with heavier papers and more paste with delicate papers. It just makes sense—after all, you wouldn't let a wrestler wear your lace nightgown, would you?

Dry-Mount Adhesives

Ever used a peel-off label to do a mailing for your favorite charity? If so, then you are familiar with the sticky labels that are backed with release paper. The stickiness is due to a type of glue called dry-mount adhesive. The release paper is slick enough to resist sticking to even Auntie Bessie's cinnamon buns, but it is willing to attach itself ever so slightly to a little dry-mount adhesive—until you peel it off.

For the purpose of New Decoupage, you can buy very thin layers of dry-mount adhesive wrapped up in a roll of release paper. Look for it in crafts shops or office supply stores. Suppose you want to attach a photo of Aunt Bessie to a tray. Just roll out a section of the dry-mount adhesive, sticky side up (or you'll end up with a very sticky work surface). Place the back of the photo onto the adhesive. Trim away the excess dry-mount adhesive and release paper. Now peel away the release paper from Bessie's backside, and she's ready to be adhered to any surface.

Dry-mount adhesives are especially effective in any situation where moisture could damage an image. Antique papers; photos; and very, very thin pieces of paper can be stuck successfully, and forever, with dry-mount adhesives.

Archival Adhesives

The word "archival" does not describe a group of adhesives but rather a quality of adhesives. All the adhesives discussed in this section are available in either archival or nonarchival quality. The difference is in the pH of the adhesive. An archival product is pH neutral, meaning it is free of the acids that yellow papers. Archival adhesives will help prevent your decoupage creations from appearing to age for at least 200 years (which is probably longer than you need them to last, and no, they do not work on human skin). However, these adhesives are more expensive. On the other hand, many (including I) believe that, when it comes to paper, the less acid the better. The choice is yours, but don't worry now about choosing between all the options. Throughout this book I'll recommend what adhesive I think works best in specific situations.

OPPOSITE: *Everything here has only one purpose in life: to hold whatever it is you choose for it to hold together. You just have to decide between an archival or non-archival PVA, ready-to-mix or ready-mixed wallpaper paste or wheat paste, dry-mount adhesive or a glue gun with glue sticks. Too many choices, you say? Never.*

"but where will I work?" THE DECOUPEUR'S DREAM HOUSE

Don't get all fretted up about where you are going to find the space in your house or apartment to begin your decoupage career. You don't need to devote an entire room, a corner, or even a counter to your decoupage. Yes, I know, we've all seen pretty work spaces in pretty books, but I'd rather do my cutting as I sit comfortably in my favorite armchair listening to mezzo-sopranos. I bring along a wastebasket, keep it beside my knee, and carefully drop the waste scraps there. I don't bother to sort anything while I cut; I'd rather enjoy the music.

Then on days when I want to feel more organized, I get out my plastic bins and folders (see page 38). I spread them out on the dining room table and sort my pile of cutouts.

I do all my preparation, painting, gold-leafing, and sealing in the basement, on an old card table that I pulled from a neighbor's trash. These often messy jobs are less worrisome in a basement (or garage), and cleanup is not so mandatory. If such a space is not adequately ventilated, get a window fan or two to pull some air through while you are working and work in short shifts, so you can shut the door and let the fumes dissipate. Shutting the door also minimizes the number of times your cat is going to walk across a freshly painted surface. If you don't have a basement or garage at your disposal, try and do this work outside or open all the windows.

If you've got time and space and your children are old enough, then by all means lay out your composition wherever you like and study it for several days. Add to it, take away from it, change your mind in favor of a better idea.

If you're working on an item of furniture intended for a room in your house, the best place to create is in the room where that item will be placed; you'll know right away when something is not working. And if it's your bedroom wall that you are working on, then you'd better be in your bedroom.

Glue small objects (even small furniture) near the kitchen sink.

Running water will make cleanup a cinch. Plus you can have a cup of coffee while you keep an eye on your work as it is drying.

You should designate specific storage spots for your supplies. How large these areas need to be depends on how obsessed you become with New Decoupage. Find some old shelving for your garage or basement. On the shelves keep paints, brushes, mineral spirits, gold-leaf size, sandpapers, and cleanup rags. Dedicate a kitchen cabinet shelf for your adhesives, sponges, and glass cleaners. Keep your artbooks on a bookshelf near your favorite cutting spot. Things you find that you use a lot—scissors, templates, single-edge razor blades, paint pens, colored pencils, artist's brushes—stay together nicely in a deep plastic storage bin, which is easy to carry around with you.

LEFT: *My neighbor Charlie throws out a lot of neat stuff. Please, nobody tell him. This old toolbox of his is ideal for keeping all my paint brushes together.*

Keep an apron in that portable bin. If you turn out to be anything like me, you never know when inspiration will come or what you'll be wearing when it does. So protect your wardrobe with an inexpensive work apron.

basic gluing techniques: TWO LESSONS

Whether you've read the previous pages or not, whether you've been sent back to this page because you got yourself into a jam and really screwed up your sister's dining room table, or whether this book just dropped into your lap open at this page is not the issue. No matter how you got here, the issue is that this is the most important section in this book.

If you want to be a decoupeur, if you already are a decoupeur, if you just want to understand your friend who calls himself a decoupeur, if you hate decoupage and are looking for arguments for it not to exist, if you are married to a decoupeur and are serious about salvaging your relationship, or if you just merely don't want to regret buying this book . . . Read this chapter very carefully. It contains all the information you need to do just about anything in the realm of decoupage.

This section presents two basic lessons: gluing beneath glass and gluing on top of a surface. If you don't have the patience to read both of them very carefully, give up decoupage and watch some more television.

Gluing Beneath Glass

For this lesson you'll need a 5 × 7″ pane of clear glass (available inexpensively at your local crafts store), PVA adhesive, your images, a damp cellulose sponge, and a coffee can with a plastic lid. In addition, you may need a basin of water (see step 3) and a swimmer's towel or chamois.

1. Begin by sanding the edges of the glass. Use an 80 or 100 grade paper, or whatever you've got in the drawer. You're not aiming for a perfectly smooth surface, just taking some precautions.

2. Once you're satisfied that you aren't going to cut yourself, make certain that the glass is also clean. Now spread a lot of glue evenly

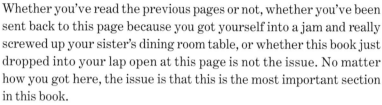

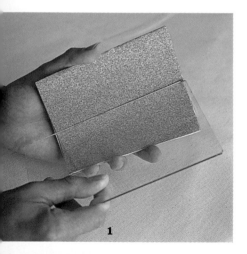

onto the glass. Use about as much as you could hold in your cupped palm. Yes, that much. And no, I'm not being paid by the makers of Elmer's (although that's what I recommend you use).

3. You must add an extra step that I call *relaxing* (and it has nothing to do with soaking in the tub) if you are dealing with an image that has colored ink on both sides of the paper. Actually, it is about soaking, but instead of soaking yourself, you are going to soak your paper images in a basin of water. This saturates the fibers in the paper with moisture, relaxing them to the point that they won't "fight" when they contact the PVA. PVA likes to be in charge and if your paper fibers are relaxed it will have an easier time doing its job correctly, helping you achieve a smooth finish. The saturation point occurs at the moment the paper stops curling in the water and floats freely without wrinkles. But don't leave the image in the basin of water for too long or the water will relax not only the paper but the ink as well, ruining the image. Have extra copies of the image standing by, just in case.

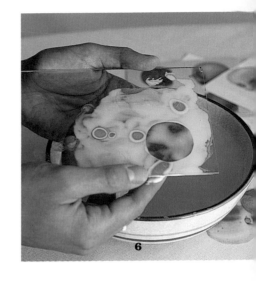

4. Pick up the image. It's not only okay to have glue on your fingers when you pick it up, it's helpful. Carefully drop the image, face down, into place. When the glue is dry and you look through the glass from the front, you should see the front of the image.

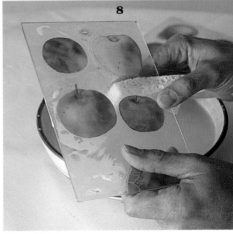

51

5. Add sufficient glue to cover the back of the image and flip the glass so that you are looking at the front.

6. Gently distribute the glue over the back of the image by using the pads of your fingers—never use your nails, lest you rip the image. Work out from the center, forcing out any pockets of air.

7. Once the air bubbles are gone, stop; don't risk tearing the image. Don't worry about leaving too much glue between the glass and the image, because it will dry clear. In fact, the more glue you work with, the easier it will be to get rid of the bubbles. Trust me.

8. Once you've got all your images in place, wipe up some of the excess glue with a water-dampened (not saturated or wet) sponge. Be careful not to disturb your images; wipe around them. It's okay to leave behind a thin film of glue, both on the glass and the backside of the image. Now rest the glass face down on the top of the coffee can (the plastic lid will prevent scratches on the glass).

9. After the glue is completely dry (this could happen within an hour if your paper is thin and it's not a humid day, or it might take overnight if you're using a heavier paper on a rainy day—you'll know

because the white glue will have turned crystal clear) you are now ready to choose a background. You might create a collage with several images, or just choose a nice wrapping paper to cover the entire back. Clean away the rest of the glue with a glass cleaner and paper towels so you can see what you're doing. Then hold the glass in front of various papers and decide what is going to look best.

10. Using the glass pane as your guide, cut the background wrapping paper to the exact size needed with an Olfa or Exacto knife.

11. Using the gluing techniques you mastered in steps 2 through 7, apply the background paper and get rid of the air bubbles.

12. Clean away excess glue from the front of the glass before you put it face down to dry on the coffee can.

13. Put your work in a frame and hang it up for all to see.

There are two important things to remember when gluing under glass. First, when working the paper into place and removing air bubbles, don't press too hard or you may permanently damage your work, and I don't mean only tearing the image, although that may happen. Excessive pressure can also remove too much glue. The glue-less areas will be shiny streaks between the glass and the image. These streaks are especially offensive when you look at the piece on the oblique. So leave hard bubble pushers—like credit cards, spoons, and your fingernails—out of this. Use only the pads of your fingers, and keep your touch firm but light.

Second, don't use a wet sponge to clean up extra glue; use a damp sponge. If a wet sponge touches the edges of the paper image, water might seep in between glass and image causing unsightly channels to appear after the work dries. Just in case that happens, a good thing to have on hand is a piece of swimmer's towel. If you've never seen one, ask any kid who swims. He or she is likely to display a bunch in designer colors. They look to me like colorized, synthetic versions of the chamois we used to use to dry our Chevrolets. Use either a piece of swimmer's towel or a chamois to soak up excess water.

Gluing under clear glass is much easier than most people think. My advice to you is to experiment and learn from your mistakes and successes. Choose and use products that work well for you. If you simply apply yourself to the task at hand and are willing to risk some minor failures at first, your continued efforts will pay off.

It took me years to figure out what's shown on these two pages. Ever since I got my first paste-pot, I've been collecting information on how to glue something perfectly onto the top of an object (and I'll bet you have too) so no doubt it's tempting to think we know all there is to know about this aspect of decoupage. But hold on—if you take a few minutes to study this lesson carefully, you just might learn something. So pick up your scissors, some wrapping paper, an old mustard jar, some Elmer's, and your brayer, and take it all to your kitchen sink. It's going to take about 5 minutes and make the rest of your decoupage career a lot easier, and that's a heck of a good thing.

Adhering Images to the Top of a Surface

1. Relax the paper in a bowl or basin of warm water until it is saturated, following the instructions on page 51. While the paper is relaxing, spread your adhesive mixture evenly onto the surface with a sponge brush. Use your hands if your only brush has just this moment fallen behind the refrigerator.

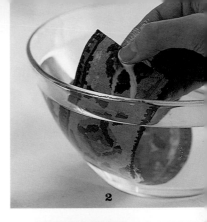

2. Remove the paper from the water and wait 10 to 15 seconds for the excess water to drip off before placing it into position.

3. Now smooth the paper flat with either a brayer or the pads of your fingers. Fingers and brayers should be wet with water and glue so they won't stick to the paper.

4. Once you've got the paper smooth and into position, clean away the excess adhesive carefully with a damp sponge. It's okay to use the sponge to remove excess adhesive from the paper but be careful not to apply too much pressure. A light film of adhesive is okay to leave behind. Once the paper has dried, this excess adhesive might appear cloudy, but the polyurethane finish will return it to clear.

5. After allowing your project to dry thoroughly, apply two coats of an acrylic polyurethane with a 1″ sponge brush following the manufacturer's instructions. Let dry.

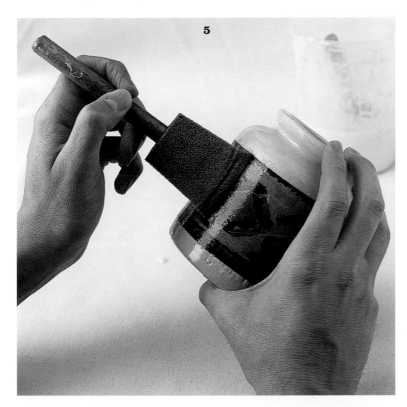

the finality of finishing:

PRESERVING YOUR PLACE IN HISTORY

Sealing a work of decoupage with polyurethane protects it from scratches, dust, and oxidation. It can also give your work a high-sheen finish and, if you use several coats, even lend depth to the finished piece. But sealing is not always necessary; in fact, many times you will want to leave a work unsealed because a sealant would unwantedly alter the look of the piece. The finish of any sealer—be it matte, semigloss, or high gloss—will bring its own sheen, as will the amber tones of varnishes and shellacs. In addition, absorbent papers can soak up sealant and, as a result, actually change color right before your eyes. You might be lucky and really like the new color, or it might make you sick.

When deciding whether to seal a piece, first consider its end use. Is your tray intended to bear the burden of Cousin Ida's gin and tonics or is it merely going to hang on the wall? If it's going to get used, it needs to get sealed; serving trays, footstools, furniture, floors, refrigerators, cabinets, and other such things should be sealed.

Next, consider the aesthetic quality of your work of art, because, as noted, any sealer will import a specific look. If you've got a cachepot that's just going to sit on the mantle and you like the natural finish of the handmade papers you used, why muck it up with polyurethane? On the other hand, you might have antique on the brain, and a coat or two of amber-colored shellac would instantly age the piece. Be sure to experiment, since different sealants provide different sheens and color characteristics. In general, oil-based products tend to turn golden and mellow with multiple coats and age (unlike your spouse). Acrylic sealants dry clear and are not expected to darken over time. I say "expected" because they haven't been on the market for a real long time and I'm from Missouri, the "Show Me" state.

Old Decoupage was sealant happy. In some cases, thirty to forty coats were recommended for one small project. I've met some frustrated decoupeurs who are still trying to do this—in tiny work spaces, windows sealed. The fumes from all that sealant could account for their obsession with so many coats, just a case of old-fashioned brain fry.

Even for those eternally committed to protecting their decoupage creation, thirty coats is downright loony, twenty coats is overdoing it, and even ten coats will get you bumped from my dinner invitation list. You want to protect your work from scratches—not Hurricane Andrew, cosmic radiation, or the *Ebola* virus.

In my opinion, a sealant overdose leaves your creation heavy and ugly. In my studio the only time we apply more than two coats of an acrylic-based polyurethane is when we have numerous layers of paper, over which coats of sealant will help you level the surface, or if we expect the piece to be very heavily used. If you decide to apply a third coat, sand the second coat lightly with a Grade 400 sandpaper. Then wipe the sanded surface with a water-dampened sponge or tack cloth before applying the third coat.

My thinking is this: If two or three coats of polyurethane will protect a floor in a new house (and that is the number many manufacturers recommend), you don't need many more to protect a floral tray; I don't care who you're inviting to tea.

For the purpose of New Decoupage, I use acrylic- and oil-based polyurethanes almost exclusively. I rarely use shellac or varnish as they're yellow to begin with and the color only deepens with age. They are also messy if the humidity is high and can take forever to dry. And forget lacquer—this is the new age and this is New Decoupage.

Polyurethane is available in two liquid forms: oil- and acrylic-based. Each is available in a formulation to provide a gloss, semi-gloss, or matte finish. Whatever you do, don't mix an oil-based polyurethane with an acrylic-based polyurethane. It's like mixing oil and water. Stick with one kind, at least until the finish is dry.

Acrylic-based polyurethane always dries clear and hard, even though it looks milky in the can and when first applied. As I mentioned, too many coats of an oil-based polyurethane imparts a mellow, golden tinge to finished work. Some people like the look, but I usually don't.

If I decide on a high-gloss, protective finish, my rule of thumb is this: Begin with two coats of acrylic polyurethane. Use additional coats whenever multiple layers of paper will benefit from the leveling effect of several coats. Finish with one or two coats of high-gloss oil-based polyurethane. The shine is better and the finish is beautifully smooth. Two coats, even three, will not cause serious yellowing.

One of the neat things about polyurethane is that the sheen of the last coat you apply is the effect you get. So why not start out with a high-gloss polyurethane for the first coat. See if you like it. If you don't, use semigloss for the second coat. When it dries, you'll have a semigloss finish. If that's not your fancy, go right on to a coat of the matte finish; it's the last coat that counts. Because brands vary, follow the manufacturer's recommendation about drying time.

Applying Polyurethane

Acrylic-Based Polyurethane. I've found the best way to apply acrylic-based polyurethane is to use an inexpensive disposable sponge brush, which costs less than a buck at the local hardware store. Select a brush size based on the size of your project; a ½-inch brush is fine for a plate; a 2½-inch brush is better for a piece of furniture.

To begin the process of applying acrylic-based polyurethane, order Chinese food, primarily dishes like egg-drop soup, each of which will be delivered in a tall plastic container with a lid. Eat the soup. Clean out the container. Store the acrylic-based polyurethane in the container. Why? Because unless you're very careful in opening the metal can of sealer that comes from the paint store, you'll probably damage the lid, making it difficult to reseal the can. Air gets in and the polyurethane gets gooky. So store what you need in egg-drop soup containers or other inexpensive plastic containers. It's okay to leave your brush in the container with the polyurethane. If you do, you're ready to polyurethane at all times—no searching for the brush, which you never have to clean. Keep the lid on when you aren't using the sealer. But if you want to clean the brush, acrylic polyurethane is water soluble; all you have to do is rinse the brush thoroughly with water.

When applying acrylic polyurethane, remember James Bond. He drank his vodka martinis stirred, not shaken. Acrylic-based polyurethanes should always be stirred, not shaken—shaking creates air bubbles. After stirring, brush the sealer on slowly and evenly, preferably while listening to a Haydn string quartet.

Manufacturers of both oil and acrylic polyurethanes will tell you to sand between every coat and to use an expensive china bristle brush for the best finish. But I like to apply two initial coats of acrylic polyurethane to make sure that the paper images are completely covered. If you attempt to sand after the first coat you will occasionally sand into the paper images. So, first two coats of acrylic, then sand lightly with Grade 400 sandpaper (this sanding will remove any dust particles or dog hairs that have settled onto the finish as it is drying and is also useful to even the polyurethane finish), then a coat of oil-based polyurethane, then sand with Grade 400 paper, then a finishing coat of oil-based poly. A tack cloth is very effective at removing the sanding "dust" but a damp sponge does a decent enough job, too. I don't always have a tack cloth ready. I always have a damp sponge at the kitchen sink. But be careful. Once you've used your kitchen sponge as a tack cloth, it's not a good idea to continue using it on your dishes; make it a part of your decoupage tool box instead. And I get more than acceptable results using a 1-inch sponge brush. Sure, you should always read the manufacturer's instructions for whatever information you can learn about how their product is supposed to behave, but to slavishly follow those instructions isn't always required. There's always an ideal way to do things, but I think the New Decoupage message is "this works, too" *and* it's not so expensive *and* it's a heck of a lot easier. Namely, something that you can accomplish.

Oil-Based Polyurethane. Applying oil-based polyurethane is exactly the same as applying acrylic-based polyurethane, but don't store it with a sponge brush in any plastic containers. It will simply eat through your brush. And, if you use it, you *must* open a window. The fumes are harmful. So why use the oil-based product at all, you ask? The finish it provides is different. It's shinier and smoother than that of even the best high-gloss acrylic. But when using it, follow the rules: Open the windows, work fast, and then leave the room while it dries. Better yet, use oil-based polyurethane outside. And while it's drying, walk around the block to your neighborhood restaurant and order a frosty vodka martini—stirred, not shaken.

Curing

Once you've sealed your work with polyurethane, you must not only let the sealant dry completely, but also let it cure. This takes longer than you think. A polyurethane finish will dry to the touch in just a few hours, but just because it's dry doesn't mean it's cured. Check the label. Some brands take days, even weeks, to cure. Oil-based products take a lot longer to cure than acrylic-based products. Until your creation is completely cured, don't attempt using it for any purpose other than decorative. Put it up on a shelf and admire it.

Caring for the Finish

Think of your polyurethaned piece as you think of a wood coffee table. Use coasters with it, clean up spills, and wipe the piece dry; never let water or any liquid sit directly on the finish. When it gets dusty, polish the piece with furniture polish. If you don't treat your coffee table that well, give this book to a friend and become an ice-hockey player.

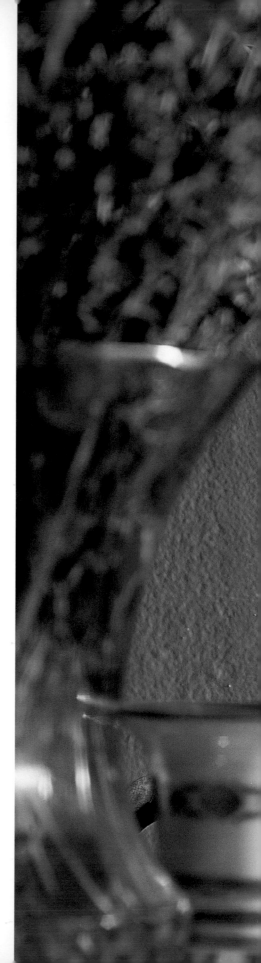

on your mark, get set, go!

Now that you understand the basics, it's time to decoupage. Parts II and III contain a range of projects, from small decorative accents to whole walls and ceilings. Once you've mastered a few of these, you may be dreaming up your own new ideas faster than the glue dries on your last project.

PART **TWO**

small stuff— decorative accessories and objets d'art

S mall decoupage pieces are important for two really good reasons. First, it's easier to practice your decoupage skills on something small. Second, small stuff is significant—decorative accessories are an essential part of any room interior, unless of course you're a minimalist, and who the heck is a minimalist? Do you know a minimalist? Or perhaps I should ask, do you know a happy minimalist? Objets d'art are great to have. Collect them, store them, rearrange them, pack and unpack them on a dull winter night—it's the one fetish I support. And if you still don't have enough of them (objets d'art, that is), New Decoupage is the ticket to many, many more. ✂ The small projects found here are a nod to the traditional world of decoupage, but even here I've played around with tradition until it met my needs; you can too. I'm not bad-mouthing tradition: Many of the objects created in my studio are, in fact, very traditional.

Images from classical artists like Watteau and Fragonard abound. So do images of old Scottish golfers putting around St. Andrews, Napoleon on his charger, Versailles costume balls, and our Blessed Lady surrounded by the heavenly host. And while all of these are beautiful, they certainly aren't the limit to what you can do. ✂ Check out the photograph on the left. It combines the cartoon world of Walt Disney with some good old American cheesecake (yes, that's really Debbie Reynolds

on the fingertip of Prince Charming). And what's wrong with that? Be it traditional or scandalous, the only limit is your imagination and your sense of what your friends and relatives will find humorous, engaging, ridiculous, offensive, silly, or profound. ✂ I've ranked the difficulty of the projects that follow by their order of appearance. The easiest come first, while the subsequent projects are more complex. So read through them in order. We'll both be glad that you did.

decoupage plates

New Decoupage is about limitless possibilities. So, it may seem kind of weird to focus first on a decoupage project that most people associate with traditional decoupage . . . the plate. But it made sense for me to start here because there are a number of techniques involved in creating decoupage plates that when mastered become the basis for pursing all those other limitless possibilities. Plus, if you make a complete mess of the thing, you can soak it all off in your sink, and no one will be the wiser. Making a plate is not like starting your decoupage career doing your living room ceiling. Screw that up and someone's bound to notice. "Say, what happened up there? Cat get caught in the fan?"

But why belabor mistakes? Decoupage is not that difficult, and just because there are a lot of steps here doesn't mean that creating a decoupage plate is difficult. Nothing that is covered here requires any skills beyond those of a beginner. And for those of you with really short attention spans, I've divided all the information into three different plate projects. First a really, really simple step, getting a central image into place and then adding some hand-painted decorative details. Followed by a plate with a pretty simple wrapping paper border. Then we tackle a plate that involves some gold leaf application. Finally, I'll show you how to accomplish a protective and professional finish on the backside of any plate. And what's more, you can complete all three plates in just 7 days—and you know from your Sunday School classes what can be created in just 6 days! So relax, be patient, and pay attention. Don't hurry, take your time, and by the end of the week you'll be amazed at your accomplishments.

1. SELECT AND SIZE YOUR IMAGE

The easiest way to do this is to hold the plate over the artwork you want to use. Look at the art through the glass plate to determine if it is the correct size and scale for the plate. If everything looks good, you are ready to cut out the image. If you want to reduce, enlarge, or otherwise change your image, refer to the section on laser copying for advice (page 42).

2. LINES TO GUIDE YOU

We made this nifty template out of clear plastic by having it cut to the exact size of the base of the octagonal plate which we were using. You can do the same on your own with a sheet of mylar and a pair of scissors to fit any size or shape of plate you might be using. If you're working on a round plate you can use a compass to determine the exact size of template that you need. After creating your template, hold it firmly in position on top of your image and trace around it with a pencil. Don't do this with an ink pen; you're just asking for trouble if you do because the ink can smear and you might end up with unsightly ink on the edge of your image. A lead pencil line is less obvious if it sneaks past your quality control.

3. CUTTING OUT THE IMAGE

Use a pair of scissors with a long blade here. Cut each side of the octagon with one steady stroke, and cut along the inside edge of the pencil line. If you're cutting round or oval shapes, remember to feed the paper into a steady open blade instead of making several small cuts all the way around (see page 32). Oh, come on, don't be so vain . . . wear your glasses.

4. RELAXING THE PAPER

This was already covered in the two gluing lessons, and I'll bet 72% of you skimmed through all that boring technical stuff and, as a result, don't understand why the image is floating in a bowl of water. If that's the case, go back to page 51 and find out why we're doing this.

5. GLUE THE IMAGE INTO POSITION

Apply a copious amount of PVA (white glue) to the underside of the plate. Don't be stingy; use a palmful. Retrieve the paper from the water and then apply it face down onto the back of the plate so that you can see the front of the image through the glass as you are looking at the front of the plate. Now, apply another palmful of glue to the backside of the image; this extra glue will prevent your fingers from sticking to the image as you work it into place and smooth out the air bubbles. Using the pads of your fingers, gently press out the air bubbles, always moving your fingers from the center of the image towards the edges. Once the image is in position and all the bubbles are gone, clean away the excess glue with a damp sponge. Make sure it's not wet. Wet is bad; wet is watery; and water can seep in between the image and the plate, which will look as bad as the dreaded air bubbles. Let the glue dry completely.

DAY ONE
Gluing a central image onto a plate

WHAT YOU'LL NEED

CLEAR GLASS PLATE (YOU CAN GET THEM ROUND, OVAL, OR OCTAGONAL AT MOST CRAFTS STORES)

PVA ADHESIVE (LIKE ELMER'S)

CELLULOSE SPONGE

SCISSORS

IMAGE

LEAD PENCIL

BASIN OF WATER

CLEAR, PLASTIC MYLAR

WHAT YOU'LL NEED

FINE- AND MEDIUM-NIB
GOLD PENS

STRAIGHTEDGE

PAINT THINNER

PAPER TOWELS OR COTTON
BALLS

BLACK LATEX PAINT

½″ ARTIST'S BRUSH

1. OUTLINE THE IMAGE WITH YOUR FINE- OR MEDIUM-NIB GOLD PEN

It's up to you how wide you want this border to be. For that matter, this whole step is optional, but I think it looks good and it's not hard.

2. DRAWING AN OUTSIDE BORDER

With the medium-nib gold pen create a border along the ridge of the plate. And don't be too fussy . . . free hand is okay, unless you're shaky and can't re-member *anything* that you were up to last night. When the pen offers a little more gold than you had in mind, don't panic. Keep some paint thinner in an old pickle jar, and you can easily clean up spills with a cotton ball or bit of pa-per towel. Don't forget to put the lid back on the paint thinner when you're done to contain the fumes . . . there are enough wacky decoupeurs out there already.

When deciding what to draw, take a good, hard look at the image you're trying to enhance. You might be able to echo a design motif in the original image, say a leaf or a pattern on a piece of clothing that is depicted in the image. The effect can be very pleasing.

3. ADD SOME DECORATIVE DRAWING

If you're now about the put this book down because you're saying to yourself, "I can't draw," just go out into the world and see what's passing for art. I guess modern art is more about self-expression than it is about following traditional forms. Which is a fancy way of saying it's okay to draw outside the lines. So, don't get down on yourself; if you're not up for re-creating your favorite flower, you can just scribble away. You'll be surprised how pleasing the effect of a common doodle can be. Have a ball; or, if you're feeling more restrained, draw precise geometric shapes; pretend you can write in Chinese; or write secret messages to your friends. I once created an obscene plate, and it is either a testimony to my incoherent penmanship or the jaded indifference of my friends (not to mention the failure of my staff to examine the plate closely before shipping it away) that no one ever noticed. I wonder who has it now, proudly displayed on their breakfront.

4. PAINT THE BACKGROUND BLACK

Allow your gold ink drawings to dry for 15 to 20 minutes before you add the black background. If you haven't skimped on your paint, two coats will usually be enough to achieve an opaque finish. Allow 2 hours drying time between each coat. And allow the final coat to dry overnight before proceeding.

5. FIXING MISTAKES

If you wake up to a paint run, carefully remove the dried paint with a straight-edge razor blade. Hold it flat against the glass to prevent scratches.

6. CREATING A HAND-PAINTED BORDER ALONG THE EDGE OF THE PLATE

Here, forget the freehand . . . you need some guidance. If you're having trouble holding the ruler straight, here's how to make yourself one of these handy little tools: just glue a straight piece of wood onto an old ruler at the distance you want your borders to be, and you don't have to worry anymore about what you did the night before.

7. Now use your new tool and add the exterior border. Just follow Steps 1 through 4 on these very pages.

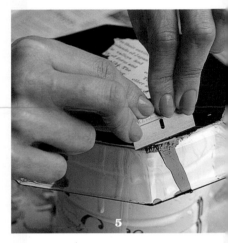

KEEP YOUR EYE ON THE PLATE AS IT'S DRYING

Here's what can happen: the outside edges usually dry faster than the inside of the plate and this can trap an air bubble near the joint of central image and wrapping paper. If this happens, push the bubble toward the center of the plate, behind the central image. It's the only place you can push it because the outside edge is already dry. This doesn't get rid of the air bubble, but it effectively hides it from everybody in your husband's family who are always looking for reasons why he shouldn't have married you.

1. CHOOSING AND CUTTING A WRAPPING PAPER BORDER

Once the central image is completely dry you are ready to choose and apply the wrapping paper border. At this point take some time and look at the plate with various background papers. This is the easiest way to find the paper that looks the absolute best. Position the plate exactly where you think it looks good on the wrapping paper and then cut an octagonal piece at least ½″ larger than the plate. Still holding the plate in position, cut seams into the background paper at each bend in the octagon.

2. ADHERING A WRAPPING PAPER BORDER

Cover the entire backside of the plate with a palmful of PVA adhesive. Position the wrapping paper face down onto the glue and spread another palmful onto the backside of the paper. Turn the plate to face you and begin to work out the excess glue.

3. TRIMMING THE EDGES

It's a good idea to trim away the excess paper before it gets too wet. At the start, the wrapping paper hasn't absorbed a lot of moisture from the glue and it is easier to cut. With a sharp pair of scissors, simply cut along the edge of the plate.

4. FINISH REMOVING THE AIR BUBBLES

Once it's trimmed exactly to size, you can concentrate on removing any remaining air bubbles. A damp sponge and running water is handy at this point to clean the face of the plate, allowing you to inspect your progress as you move toward a perfect finish. After you've gotten rid of the last bubble, place the plate face down on an empty coffee can and allow it to dry thoroughly, usually overnight. You'll know it's completely dry when the whiteness of the glue is completely gone. And don't worry if the glue under the central image turns white again during this whole process. That's normal; it, too, will dry clear.

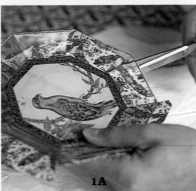

WHAT YOU'LL NEED

WRAPPING PAPER

SCISSORS

PVA

CELLULOSE SPONGE

DAY FOUR
Gilding the lily

Why does everyone seem to think of gilding the lily as a negative? Gold is simply the best color going so why not learn how to use it. Learn how to gild and there'll be no stopping you. Easter will never be the same.

WHAT YOU'LL NEED

ACRYLIC POLYURETHANE

1″ SPONGE BRUSH

GOLD LEAF SIZE

COMPOSITION GOLD LEAF (OR THE REAL THING, IF YOU HAVEN'T SPENT ALL YOUR DOLLARS ON OTHER HOW-TO BOOKS)

COTTON BALLS OR COSMETIC BRUSH

1. PROTECTING WHAT YOU'VE ALREADY DONE

A coat of acrylic polyurethane is essential to protect your work before gold leafing. Apply an even coat over the entire backside, yes all of the paper, paint, and glass. The milky-colored stuff dries clear. Allow this to dry for at least 2 hours.

2. APPLYING THE SIZING

Before gilding you need to apply a quick-dry synthetic gold size varnish. Apply just one coat over the clear glass. I know what you're thinking, you're thinking the size in the photo is being applied to the back side of the paper, not the glass. Well that was intentional. Because, depending on the humidity you'll have to wait 45 minutes to an hour until the size achieves the appropriate "tack." Test this by touching the size on the paper where it's not going to show. Who wants to see your fingerprints on the glass? You see, it's a good idea to have a small area of the size on the backside of the paper where you can test it for the appropriate tack. It should feel like the fingers of your sister's 3-year-old who just dropped a saliva-slick lollipop on your new blouse. Now you're ready to gild. So try to forget about your blouse and finish the plate.

3. GILDING

People go on and on about this, professing the importance of special tools and special techniques. They go to classes and call themselves pros, and I suppose that's all very valid. But it also intimidates a lot of people new to the idea of gilding. Well, I am here to tell you, don't worry if you're just taking up gilding. What we're doing here, you can handle. Just pick up a corner of the flimsy stuff with your fingers and drop it into place. Don't do this by an open window as the slightest breeze is going to thwart you. Then, with the palm of your hand press it gently down into place. All you want to do is to get the gold to stick evenly to the tacky size. If it moves around at all, that

means that the size wasn't tacky enough when you applied the gold leaf. Next time, let it dry a little more. When the tack is good, burnish it with a cotton ball or cosmetic brush. Then allow it to dry a minimum of 4 hours.

4. FOUR HOURS LATER

Repeat Steps 1 through 3. There's not any getting around this second application of gold leaf, if you want complete coverage. Allow this second application to dry overnight.

DAY FIVE

Brush away the excess gold leaf and add another layer of protection by applying two coats of acrylic polyurethane to the backside of the gilded areas. Allow this to dry overnight. As this wasn't a very busy day, maybe you should vacuum the house.

DAY SIX
Finishing the backside of a decoupage plate

WHAT YOU'LL NEED

CONSTRUCTION PAPER

SCISSORS

COFFEE CAN WITH PLASTIC LID

PVA ADHESIVE

1″ SPONGE BRUSH

BLACK LATEX PAINT

WIDE-NIB GOLD PEN

SINGLE-EDGED RAZOR BLADE

MEDIUM TO FINE SANDPAPER

ACRYLIC POLYURETHANE

1. CUTTING A PROTECTIVE CONSTRUCTION PAPER BACK
Resting the paper and plate on your coffee can, cut an oversized piece of construction paper, turning the plate as you go.

2. APPLYING THE CONSTRUCTION PAPER TO THE BACK
Brush an even but thin layer of PVA onto the back of the plate. Press the construction paper into place firmly with both hands.

3. TRIM THE EXCESS
Turn the plate over and vertically trim off the excess around the edges with your scissors.

4. SKIP AN APPOINTMENT WITH YOUR THERAPIST
Turn the place face down on the coffee can and take out the aggression that you're feeling about our federal government by smoothing the paper flat with your ex-husband's credit card and hope he's losing some sleep looking for it.

5. CONTROLLING THE SEAMS AND EDGES OF THE PLATE
Add some additional glue to the seams and edges. This is helpful as the paper has a slight overlap at the seams and the additional glue will give you a smoother finish. Allow this to dry for 20 minutes.

6. FINE TUNING THE EDGES
Carefully trim the edge with a fresh, i.e., new, straight-edged razor blade. A new blade is a must for every plate. Reason: paper isn't kind to razor blades. A blade that's been used—even once—will not give you a clean, smooth cut. So buy the blades in boxes by the hundreds; you'll only spend 6 or 7 cents per plate. Your talents are worth that!

7. GETTING IT EXACT
With a medium to fine grade of sandpaper, carefully sand the edge smooth to the touch. But don't sand too hard or you might sand away some of the background paint or paper.

8. SAFE NOT SORRY
Whether you've sanded too vigorously or not, thoroughly paint around the edge of the plate with a wide-nib gold pen. This minimizes any imperfections.

9. PAINTING THE BACK
After allowing the construction paper to thoroughly dry (4 to 6 hours) place the plate face down on the coffee can and paint the back of the plate with a black latex enamel paint, usually 2 to 3 coats, allowing 2 hours drying time between each coat. Once it's covered and dry, you are ready to sign your creation (use a fine-nib gold pen), and finish it off with 2 protective coats of acrylic polyurethane. Allow this to dry overnight. No we are not done yet. But almost.

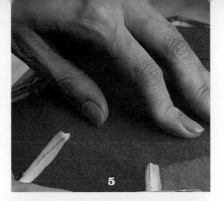

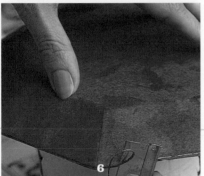

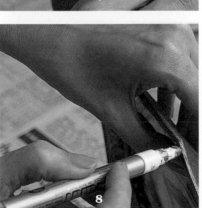

The "Day of Rest" has finally arrived but you're probably too anxious not to pick up your decoupage plate to admire the end-result of all your discipline and hard work. And, putting all admonishments against working on this day aside, you decide there'd be no real harm in cleaning the front of it. Using a glass cleaner, paper towels, and a single-edged razor blade (for any tough bits of glue) you effectively clean your creation and thereby satisfy yourself of both your talents and recent accomplishments. You can now, with no small measure of contentment, hurry off to your church, temple, or mosque where you see for the first time the new decoupaged offering plate that a crafty friend donated to your house of worship because she read this book before you did.

DAY SEVEN
Worship and Accomplishments

WHAT YOU'LL NEED

PAPER TOWELS
GLASS CLEANER
SINGLE-EDGED RAZOR BLADE
BIBLE OR KORAN

trivet

Traditionally, trivets are some of the world's most boring items, often taking the form of plain slabs of wood or cork. Here's an easy solution if you are afflicted with BTS . . . boring trivet syndrome. This project calls for a ¼-inch-thick glass disk, which you can have cut at the local glass shop. Just ask the salesperson to cut a piece to the size you want your trivet to be, and make sure you ask to have the edges sanded smooth.

Since you already know how to glue under glass, you already know most everything you need to know to create a trivet like the one pictured. This piece features a single gorgeous image with an equally gorgeous message: "ΘΕΟΘΕΝ ΑΥΞΑ ΝΟΜΑΙ" (Flowers and meadows grow from the gods). I decided not to risk messing it up with a border drawn by yours truly, or anything else. But, hey, if you're feeling creative, make this as complicated as your last decoupage plate. The process is the same up to a point.

1. If necessary, relax images in a basin of water. Following the instructions for gluing beneath glass (see page 50), use your fingers to spread PVA adhesive on the glass disk and then apply the image to the glass. For ideas on how to embellish the trivet, see instructions for Decoupage Plates.

2. Let dry overnight and back with construction paper, as described on page 74. After the backing paper has dried for approximately 20 minutes, trim the edge clean with a single-edge razor blade.

3. Let the paper dry thoroughly (at least 3 hours). Using a 1″ sponge brush, paint the back of the trivet with latex enamel paint. The color's up to you, and don't think too much about it—who's going to see the bottom?

4. For a more sophisticated touch, elevate the trivet on 4 small, round feet, which you can get ready-made at a crafts store or through a mail-order catalogue. These can just be glued into place with the PVA or a hot-glue gun. If you do use the feet, you really should paint them to match the underside of the trivet—tots peering at them from eye level will ask you why you didn't. Apply 2 coats of acrylic-based polyurethane.

5. Prepare a tuna casserole, invite friends to dinner, and casually remove the tuna casserole dish from the trivet. Await inevitable raves about the beautiful trivet, which will be a welcome distraction if the casserole is a bust.

WHAT YOU'LL NEED

IMAGES

BASIN OF WATER

PVA ADHESIVE

¼″ THICK GLASS DISK

CELLULOSE SPONGE

CONSTRUCTION PAPER

SINGLE-EDGE RAZOR BLADE

GRADE 400 SANDPAPER

1″ SPONGE BRUSH

LATEX ENAMEL PAINT

4 WOODEN FEET (OPTIONAL)

HOT-GLUE GUN WITH GLUE STICKS (OPTIONAL)

ACRYLIC-BASED POLYURETHANE

TUNA CASSEROLE

mantel urns

With an eye toward getting some great bargains, you go to a flea market with a friend. But everything that isn't broken is Park Avenue–priced. The only thing you've found that's inexpensive and not broken is a tin urn. You decide the primary reason it hasn't been snapped up is because it's so ugly it turns your stomach, but you pick it up anyway—perhaps because the shape of the thing has got some integrity. But your friend jumps back. "That's not an urn," she says, "that's an affront to humanity." Well, she may be right, but you don't despair. You just politely tell your friend that New Decoupage can bring that urn back from the dead, and what's more, you know quite a bit about how to do just that. Her eyebrow raises as you give her a sly grin. You pay the dealer a dollar and your friend plays Lotto with her dollar. Who's the loser here?

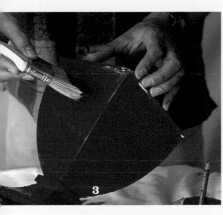

1. Following the instructions beginning on page 24, prepare the surface of the urn. Using a brush, apply 2 coats of alkyd primer to the outside of the urn. Let each coat dry completely. Apply 2 coats of red latex paint. Let dry completely, 2 to 4 hours, per coat.

2. Mix darker red pigment into glazing compound. I suppose you want me to tell you the exact colors of red we used here, but I've got to be honest; I haven't the foggiest. We rarely use a color out of the can. How can somebody in a Benjamin Moore office in Toledo come up with a color that's going to be perfect for my livingroom? You gotta mix your own . . . that's all there is to it. For some tips on the ins and outs of mixing paints, see page 113.

3. Next you're going to stipple. Sounds hard, even vaguely obscene, but it's really simple. Use a common bristle brush—2″—and instead of brushing the dark-red glazing mixture onto the surface, aim the ends of the bristles straight at the surface and bounce it on staccato-style. How much you bounce the bristles determines how much glaze gets onto the surface of the urn. Don't jump in and muck things up; practice first on a piece of cardboard. You want the density of your stipples to be consistent.

4. Allow the glaze to dry overnight and then, following steps 3–5 on page 55, apply the images. Since you can see only 2 sides of the urn at once, I suggest that you work on 2 sides at the same time. Wipe away the excess glue with a water-dampened sponge. Allow the first 2 sides to dry thoroughly before turning the urn and carrying the design around to the third and fourth sides. Sponge away excess glue. Let the second 2 sides dry overnight.

5. Using a sponge brush, apply 2 coats of acrylic-based polyurethane, letting each coat dry thoroughly. Let the polyurethane cure for 3 days before you use the urn.

WHAT YOU'LL NEED

URN

PAINT PRIMER

1″ SPONGE BRUSH

RED LATEX ENAMEL PAINT

DARK RED PIGMENT

ACRYLIC GLAZING COMPOUND

MIXING CONTAINER

2″ BRISTLE BRUSH

IMAGES

50/50 MIXTURE OF PVA ADHESIVE AND WALLPAPER PASTE

BASIN OF WATER

BRAYER

CELLULOSE SPONGE

ACRYLIC-BASED POLYURETHANE

six-sided wood-block puzzle

This is a remarkably simple project, yet it always wins raves. It makes an especially nice gift to present to little children, before they become too corrupted by computer games and contemporary music. There is something reminiscent of earlier times in a simple wood-block puzzle, and it somehow seems unnatural that only the under-5 set delight in it today. This puzzle can be cre-ated with a minimum of 4 blocks and as many as . . . well, how crazy do you want to get? The number 35 strikes me as a good cutoff, but, hey, if you're all alone on a cold winter night and you just can't figure out why, there's no reason you can't use a couple hundred. Wood blocks in various sizes are available at local crafts stores and through mail-order catalogues.

1. Assemble the blocks to form a square or rectangular shape. Make sure each image you've chosen will cover all the blocks; use the laser copier to enlarge or reduce accordingly.

Think about all 6 sides of the puzzle before you begin. We decided to make the puzzle pictured very instructive, so each of the 6 sides presents 6 of my favorite dogs.

WHAT YOU'LL NEED

WOOD BLOCKS

IMAGES

WORK SURFACE COVERED WITH NEWSPAPER

WOOD STAIN

RAG

OLFA OR X-ACTO KNIFE

ACRYLIC-BASED POLYURETHANE

ARTIST'S BRUSH

RUBBER BAND

CUTTING MAT

PVA ADHESIVE

CELLULOSE SPONGE

2. Using a brush, apply wood stain to all sides of all blocks. Use a dry rag to wipe away the excess. Yes, stain all 6 sides at once; we've got a lot to cover here and they won't really stick to the paper. Let the stained blocks dry overnight. If a bit does stick on an edge or two, just scrape the newspaper away with your fingernail (or, if you've bitten them down during a previous project, use a single-edge razor blade).

3. Using an artist's brush, apply acrylic-based polyurethane to 5 sides of each block (polyurethane will stick to the newspaper) and allow to dry for 4 hours. Then, turn the blocks over and apply the acrylic-based polyurethane onto the sixth side. Let dry overnight.

4. Now, reassemble the blocks into the chosen rectangular or square form. To keep the blocks in place and tightly pressed together, bind them around the girth with a rubber band.

5. Lay one image atop the assembled blocks, making sure it's properly positioned. With an Olfa or X-acto knife, mark all perimeter cuts that need to be made.

6. Remove the artwork to a cutting mat. With a straightedge and the knife, use the guide marks to cut the image into vertical strips. Place the first strip face up on the cutting surface. Then, using one block as a template, position that block at the top end of the strip, making sure that the edges of the block meet the edges of the strip perfectly. Make the cut necessary to create a square section of image just large enough to fit onto the face of the block. Repeat until you have apportioned the whole image.

7. Use PVA adhesive and your fingers to glue the cut-up image onto the blocks, one image per block. With a water-dampened sponge, remove excess glue. Allow to dry. Finish one entire side of the puzzle and allow to dry overnight. Using the artist's brush, apply 2 coats of acrylic-based polyurethane to all 35 blocks covered by the image. Allow to dry thoroughly then jumble the blocks. Repeat this step over six days, finishing each side of the puzzle.

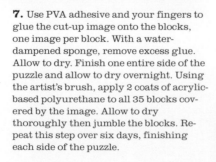

serving tray

A lot of decorative accessories just sit around looking lovely; they are, after all, objets d'art. But your decoupage creations can also be functional. Enter the serving tray. What better way to enrage your neighbor the craftsperson than by serving him or her dessert on a beautiful decoupage tray of your own superior design?

A decoupage tray can also be a great, inexpensive gift. We all have weird friends, right? And they all have birthdays, which most of them loathe or love or lie about, but never ignore. In fact, they want stuff on their birthdays. But finding the right gift can be difficult. They have everything, and what they don't have you can't provide: a real life, a million dollars, a

chateau in the south of France, eternal bliss.

But there is something you can provide . . . a customized decoupage tray, the perfect gift for that friend who is a ballet freak with a love of baseball and a fascination for horror movies. Cut out images of werewolves, slime monsters, vampires, Degas ballerinas, and the New York Yankees and arrange them in a surreal tableau that will amaze and delight your friend. Then make a second tray for yourself, on which you feature representations of your own very personal idiosyncrasies. Just be sure to show the tray to your shrink before you loan it to the Junior League for the next charity benefit.

1. PREPARE THE SURFACE

Following the instructions beginning on page 24, prepare the tray surface. Using a sponge brush, apply 2 coats of alkyd primer to the top of the tray, allowing 4 hours drying time between each coat. When completely dry, use a brush to apply 2 coats of black latex enamel paint to each side. Allow the paint to dry overnight before positioning images.

2. COMPOSE THE IMAGES

As the paint dries, think. Nothing more, just think. You're composing a scene; maybe it's the interior of a room, maybe it's the playing field at Yankee Stadium, or maybe it's just some prettily arranged ripe fruit. It's important to spend time considering the arrangement of the images.

3. TEST-APPLY THE IMAGES

Place the images into position on the tray, working from the background to the foreground. If you want, you can hold them in place with tape while you play around with different combinations.

4. ADHERE THE IMAGES

Once you're happy with your composition, use a brush to apply a 50/50 mixture of PVA adhesive and wallpaper paste onto the surface of the tray.

WHAT YOU'LL NEED

SPONGE BRUSH

PAINT PRIMER

LATEX ENAMEL PAINT

IMAGES

50/50 MIXTURE OF PVA ADHESIVE AND WALLPAPER PASTE

BASIN OF WATER

BRAYER

CELLULOSE SPONGE

FINE-NIB GOLD PEN (OPTIONAL)

ACRYLIC-BASED POLYURETHANE

OIL-BASED POLYURETHANE

GRADE 400 SANDPAPER

HANDMADE PAPER (OPTIONAL)

SCISSORS

SINGLE-EDGE RAZOR BLADE (OPTIONAL)

Then, if necessary, dip the image into the filled water basin to relax it (see page 51). Depending on the paper and how it has been treated, this may happen immediately or it may take a few minutes. When the image is relaxed, not curling or wrinkling, remove it from the water, gently shaking away the excess water. Lay the image into position. Using a wet brayer and applying even pressure, roll out the excess glue.

5. CLEAN AWAY EXCESS GLUE

Use a water-dampened sponge to remove excess wet glue while you're working. Don't glue a wet image on top of another wet image; it will create a slippery mess. Be patient and let an image dry thoroughly before you glue on another that touches it. And be flexible; don't stay wedded to your original design if something else suddenly looks better.

6. APPLY DECORATIVE DETAILS

If you want, with the fine-nib gold pen, embellish the tray with some decorative painting—swirls, words, doodles, geometrics, graffiti. The simplest designs can be striking in this context.

7. FINISH THE FRONT OF THE TRAY

Once the images and embellishments are dry, use a sponge brush to apply 2 coats of acrylic-based polyurethane to the front of the tray, allowing 2 hours drying time between each coat. After

about 4 hours, or when the second coat has thoroughly dried, you can begin to build layers of oil-based polyurethane—as many as you need, depending on how many layers of paper you have and how smooth you want the surface to be. If small bumps or imperfections develop in the finish, between coats sand it gently with Grade 400 sandpaper. Remove the dust before you apply the next coat.

8. FINISH THE BACK OF THE TRAY

You might want to paint, sign, and polyurethane the underside of the tray. Or you might want to make it a little fancier by applying a handmade paper.

To do this, first paint the underside a color similar to that of the color of the paper you will use. Allow the paint to dry overnight. Use scissors to cut an oval from the handmade paper that is slightly larger than the base of the tray. Using a brush, apply an even layer of adhesive mixture over the entire painted underside of the tray. Place the paper into place and roll it with a wet brayer. Press the edges up under the lip of the tray, or trim away the excess against the tray's edge after the paper has dried. Allow to dry overnight and use a sponge brush to apply 2 coats of acrylic-based polyurethane. After the acrylic coats are thoroughly dry, use a brush to apply 2 coats of oil-based polyurethane. Allow the tray to to cure for 2 weeks before using.

cachepot and decoupage eggs

USING A BRAYER

The only way to really learn the proper amount of pressure to apply when using a brayer in different situations is by trial and error. Practice with an image on a scrap of painted board or metal. Once you get a feel for it, you'll be amazed at how easy it is to strike that point between too much pressure (which tears the paper) and too little (which prevents a strong bond from developing between image and surface).

A decoupage cachepot filled with delicate decoupage eggs is a beautiful presentation, and an easy one to accomplish. Of course, you don't have to showcase the cachepot and the eggs together. Just strew the eggs around the living room, bedroom, or bathroom to add an elegant touch to your interiors, and display the cachepot on a mantle, night table, or dining room sideboard.

The decoupaging of the cachepot is simple. Actually, there's very little to discuss: You already know how to decoupage the surface, if you've read the basic gluing instructions (see page 50) or the instructions for the Serving Tray (see pages 83–85).

And you already know how to enlarge or reduce images to the exact size that you need, not to mention your highly developed skills with the Tranquil Color button of the laser copier (see pages 42–43). The muted colors of the antique book that provided the portraits I used—printed in Paris and found by a friend at a California flea market—required the soft touch of the tranquil colors.

CACHEPOT

1. Prepare the surface by following the instructions that begin on page 24.

2. Select images and, if necessary, laser-copy them to the desired size. For the cachepot shown, we used a different portrait for each side.

3. If necessary, relax the paper in a basin of water (see page 51).

4. Using a brush, apply an even layer of PVA adhesive onto one side of the cachepot; position the artwork.

5. Smooth the artwork flat with a wet brayer.

6. Wipe away excess glue with a water-dampened sponge.

7. Allow glue to dry overnight.

8. Using a sponge brush, apply 2 coats of matte-finish acrylic-based polyurethane, letting each coat dry thoroughly.

WHAT YOU'LL NEED

FOR THE CACHEPOT:

METAL CACHEPOT

IMAGES

BASIN OF WATER

PVA ADHESIVE

BRAYER

CELLULOSE SPONGE

BRISTLE BRUSH

ACRYLIC-BASED POLYURETHANE

GO WITH THE BUMPS AND DIPS

The surfaces of inexpensive metal objects are often marred with little dents or bumps. Don't try to sand down the bumps or fill in the depressions; it just won't work on metal as it does on wood and plastic. Instead, consider choosing images that enhance the antique, timeworn look. In this case, you want the cachepot to look like it has been around since Louis XVI; imperfections are expected. So simply press your image over or into the flaw, and worry about something more important. Like whatever happened to the Dauphin?

DECOUPAGE EGGS

The Russian czars had beautiful bejeweled eggs created for them by master craftsmen such as Peter Carl Fabergé. Chances are, you don't. But New Decoupage allows you to create some very special eggs of your own. They may not sell for billions of rubles, but if one breaks at least you can replace it.

1. Get the kids in the room. Kids love doing this.

2. With a straight pin, poke small holes into both ends of each egg. Gently blow out the whites and yolks into a mixing bowl.

3. Beat whites and yolks with fork until well blended. Over low heat, melt enough butter to cover the bottom of a skillet. Pour in beaten eggs and stir with the fork. With clean decoupage scissors, snip chives into the eggs. Stir slowly, until eggs are set and not runny.

4. Using a spatula, serve immediately on slices of toast.

5. Now, fortified in your efforts to re-create the eggs of the czars, lay out the images. They should be small and shaped as appropriate for conforming to the curve of an egg. The smaller the image, the easier it will be to attach. You will apply images directly to the white eggshells—there is no need to paint the eggs. The natural eggshell-white background is already perfect. Relax the images in water (see page 51). Because of the small, curved surface to which it will be glued, the paper must be completely relaxed, or it will curl up at the ends.

6. With your fingertips, spread a small amount of PVA adhesive onto an egg. Press the image firmly (but not too firmly) into place. You don't need to clean the glue from your fingers; it will help you not stick to the image. Remove excess glue with a water-dampened sponge.

7. When dry, use an artist's brush to finish with 2 coats of acrylic-based polyurethane, allowing each coat to dry thoroughly. Apply the polyurethane to one side at a time, resting the dry side on a spoon.

WHAT YOU'LL NEED

FOR THE EGGS:

KIDS

STRAIGHT PIN

EGGS

MIXING BOWL

FORK, BUTTER, SKILLET, SCISSORS, CHIVES, SPATULA, TOAST

IMAGES

BASIN OF WATER

PVA ADHESIVE

CELLULOSE SPONGE

ARTIST'S BRUSH

ACRYLIC-BASED POLYURETHANE

SPOONS

floral vase

People who have a passing knowledge of decoupage think of it as a fussy craft that occupies lonely people on cold winter nights. They look at decoupage plates and say, "That's nice." I hate it when people look at my work and say, "That's nice." I want to hear—and so do you—a great big "Wow!" This project will get you that great big "Wow" accompanied by "That's really decoupage? Are you serious?"

Yes, you are, and here's how you do it. You're going to take what you learned about gluing under glass (see page 50) and apply it to the inside of a clear glass vase. It isn't that hard, but there are a few tricks, such as this one: When creating a decoupage vase, always work from the bottom up. You don't want to interfere with artwork glued around the top as you take your arm in and out. So design and glue from the ground up.

When hunting for flower prints, look for art books featuring the great 18th- and 19th-century botanical illustrators. Such books usually contain loads of color pictures. If you want to use the finished vase for real flowers, find a plastic liner vase at a crafts store or florist; otherwise, the water you put in for the flowers will ruin your decoupage.

1. SELECT IMAGES

If you have just one or two really good images that you want to use, make several laser copies of them so they can be repeated around the vase. Because the vase does have some curves, the images, which are flat, will have to bend in some areas to adhere properly. With this in mind, try to use small or long, thin images; these will take to a curved shape easier than will a large, wide image. Or, if you must use a big image—say, a rose—use scissors to cut into the rose along the lines of the petals. When it is applied to the curved glass surface, the petals will overlap a little and conform to the shape of the vase. Whenever effecting this trick, always cut into the image at places where the image might naturally be broken up—at the juncture of a stem and flower, or between flower petals.

2. APPLY IMAGES

Using your fingers, smear gobs of glue on the interior wall of the vase, starting at the bottom, where you want to begin positioning images. With the front of the image facing you through the glass, press the image into place, working out the excess glue and smoothing the air bubbles out gently with your fingertips. Once the air bubbles have disappeared and you've cleaned away the excess glue with a water-dampened sponge, move on to the next image. Continue positioning and gluing. Don't be too fastidious about cleaning away all the glue; just go after the big globs. Once all the images are in place, let them dry completely before attempting to clean away the balance of the glue. See page 50 for complete instructions on gluing under glass.

3. GET RID OF THE REST OF THE GLUE

Using a damp sponge, carefully remove the excess glue adhering to the glass between the images. You will need to resort to a glass cleaner and paper towels to get rid of all the glue; you want the glass to be very clean before you paint. (If the images are completely dry, this thorough cleaning won't damage them.) As you clean, carefully examine the edges of all the images. Because the surface is curved, you might find a few raised edges. Fill these in with a bit of glue. This will prevent the background paint from seeping underneath them and ruining all your hard work. Once all the art is in place and dry and you've checked and corrected any raised edges, you are ready to paint the inside background color.

4. PAINT THE BACKGROUND COLOR

Using a sponge brush, evenly apply one coat of cream-colored latex enamel paint to the inside of the vase. Again, work from the bottom of the vase to the top, and it's okay to paint right over the back of the images. The application of the paint may rewet some of the glue between images and glass. If it does, don't panic; the glue will dry clear again, once the paint is dry. The number of coats you need to apply until the background is opaque depends on the paint color and quality of paint. Just keep applying coats until the paint is opaque, letting each coat dry thoroughly before applying the next. And be patient. There's not a lot of air circulation inside the vase, so the drying times will be extended. I've found it best to let the vase dry overnight between each coat.

WHAT YOU'LL NEED

IMAGES

SCISSORS

PVA ADHESIVE

CLEAR GLASS OR CRYSTAL VASE

CELLULOSE SPONGE

GLASS CLEANER

PAPER TOWELS

SPONGE BRUSH

CREAM-COLORED LATEX ENAMEL PAINT

black and white
bird vase

So you mastered the floral vase and think you know all there is to know about creating this exquisite pair of vases. Creating these vases is a simple variation of the skills mastered in the previous project, but don't jump into creating these beauties until you've carefully read the following. Yes, it's true, all the gluing and cleaning and finishing techniques you need to know haven't changed; however, a few challenges await you.

These vases were actually modeled after a pair of antique decoupage vases I saw in a Paris antiques shop. Unfortunately, at 10,000 francs apiece, I couldn't afford them and, upon my return to New York, I couldn't forget them—black and white birds just standing around in a cream background. Luckily, with New Decoupage as part of my decorating arsenal, I was able to create reproductions. To paraphrase a Noel Coward quip: All artists steal, the good ones don't get caught.

WHAT YOU'LL NEED

IMAGES

SCISSORS

PVA ADHESIVE

2 CLEAR GLASS OR CRYSTAL VASES

SYNTHETIC CELLULOSE SPONGE

GLASS CLEANER

PAPER TOWELS

SPONGE BRUSH

CREAM-COLORED LATEX ENAMEL PAINT

The most challenging part of the whole project was learning how to cut and glue a bird; the rest was easy.

When trying to apply a cutout image of a thin and spindly bird—with its small feathers, thin legs, sharp beak, and little talons—think of Thanksgiving and what we do to the bird on that day. We cut it up and serve it in pieces. Do the same thing here, pilgrim; otherwise, the entire image will curl up as soon as it comes in contact with the glue. Cut off the individual feathers that stick out, then cut away the legs and feet as well. After applying the bird torsos and allowing those to dry, it will be easy to reattach the small parts that were removed. Don't worry about getting everything back into perfect position. No one will notice. And, in the unlikely event that people do, tell them that if they knew anything about anything they'd understand that birds are by nature a bit ruffled. Then send them home to read some Noel Coward.

If you decide to tackle this project, it's a good idea to limit yourself to just two species of birds. Otherwise, you may not be able to keep track of which beak belongs to which bird. Using the multi-image function on the laser copier, you can economically laser-copy as many as you need to complete both vases (we used about forty birds to complete the large vases in the photo). And you really do need two species. One would be terribly lonely on such a big vase. Once the images are ready, follow the step-by-step instructions for the Floral Vase, which begin on page 90.

hooray for hatboxes

Closets crammed? Cupboards packed? Need more storage space? Throw out your old hats. Sound illogical? Not really. No one wears hats anymore (what a tragedy) so give them the heave-ho and save the boxes they came in. Or buy some new boxes from a crafts store or by mail-order catalogue. And (you guessed it), decoupage them. Once they're done, you store stuff in them: seed packages, tax returns, linens, old photos, dog treats. Anything. And then use the boxes to decorate your living space. This is living! Here are some design ideas:

This is a great place to keep all your cards and love letters. If it makes you happy to reminisce in a favorite chair in your living room, then use the same wallpaper that you used on your livingroom ceiling to cover the top of the box. The coordinating striped paper is perfect for the edges and sides. It will look good stored under that chair—you hardly have to move at all.

I wouldn't tell everybody what's in it, but for those of you who've had more lovers than one box can hold, create a second box with the same papers. Add a provocative Renaissance portrait and cut out and use only the flowers from that same wallpaper.

Addicted to family photos and got no time to sort them into albums? This textured box was created with a single wrap of an Anaglypta paper border. Anaglypta dates back to the Victorian Age. It's simply wallpaper with a very beautiful texture. We got this border at our local hardware store for the sides of this box. One image from an artbook and an edge made out of wrapping paper took care of the rest of this design.

This box got a little more complicated, but often things also get complicated around the dinner table. And please don't try to analyze me using the composition of the collage on top. I liked the images and I liked the way they looked together. That's how simple my philosophy of decoupage composition is. Now what's for dinner?

PART THREE

furniture and architectural decoupage

O bjets d'art are usually small. They are decorative accents, akin to seasonings in a gourmet meal, in that they enhance rather than define their surroundings. Recent popular decoupage has focused on these decorative accents, but it is interesting to note that traditional decoupage was conceived on a much larger scale. For example, the Venetian craftsmen who invented this art form applied it to large furnishings. New Decoupage seeks to reclaim this heritage, paying homage to the adage "Bigger is better." But don't get scared. Just because these projects are bigger doesn't mean that they're more difficult. By and large, the projects found in this section don't require any more skills than the ones you've already mastered creating smaller works of art. You're just going to be working on a bigger scale. ✄ If you're still feeling queasy at the idea of tackling your livingroom ceiling, relax. We're going to take an intermediary step before we serve up the walls, ceilings, and fireplaces. For now, let's just look at how New Decoupage treats ordinary furnishings. Rather than list every single piece of furniture imaginable, I've chosen a few representative pieces on which it's easy to demonstrate some new techniques. But don't limit yourself to what I've shown here; these techniques can be applied to a whole host of furnishings, from coffee tables and chairs to benches, beds, and desks. Just look around you; think creatively; let your imagination run wild. ✂ The real beauty of this large-scale approach is that it can truly transform an environment at very little cost and, in the process, give you a wonderful sense of accomplishment. How often have

you heard someone say, "I can't stand that table. It's old, ugly, and chipped. Yuck. But I can't run out and buy a new piece of furniture every day, so I guess I'll just have to live with it." Actually, you probably never heard anyone say exactly that, but I'm sure you have heard complaints to that effect. ✂ Well, if you've taken the time to practice a few decoupage techniques, you'll never have to worry about being the one who's expressing

those sentiments again. Just keep a few basic decorating ideas in mind. If you're going to transform a big piece of furniture, such as a secretary or desk, the design should be part of the overall decorating scheme for the room it will be in. Keeping

that room scheme in mind, decide in advance what colors will work best and what images might look good. Do you want the piece to blend in or stick out? Do you want it to be whimsical or serious? How do you want it to relate to the other pieces of furniture? It may be that you have six pieces of furniture in a room, and the pieces are so diverse that they are giving the room a disorganized feeling known in decorating circles as eclectic.

ABOVE: *Close inspection of this decoupaged vanity reveals a mistake: the lower-right hand corner of the lower drawer has not been correctly mitered. But the truth is, who cares?*

OPPOSITE: *There is no easier way to create an elegant ceiling for your parlour than to use Anaglypta paper. This elegant paper is pressed into countless beautiful designs, and is great for covering cracks in your walls and for obscuring imperfect ceilings in old apartments.*

ABOVE: Ora et Labora *in Latin means pray and work . . .
good advice for beginning and experienced decoupeurs. To
help pull this mantle area together, I created the design on
the cachepots with flower petals snipped from the design on
the door. Decoupage allows for easy application of design
motifs that help organize diverse spatial elements.*

It's been my experience that many rooms described as eclectic are crying out for a unifying decorative theme, which can be easily achieved through decoupage. Perhaps you will choose a floral motif or birds, or maybe you can draw everything together by using images with similar colors or a recurring abstract design. Through decoupage, you might create theme rooms. If you're religious, you can make the room "chapelesque." If you're feeling campy, decorate with Hollywood cheesecake. If you're nuts for Napoleonic France, decoupage with images and reminders of the Emperor himself. If you're a sports fan, images of your favorite games can mark the space as yours and yours alone. ✂ You get the idea—don't be limited to just reviving one dilapidated piece of furniture. Think big, and in the process delight your friends, confound your enemies, and amuse yourself.

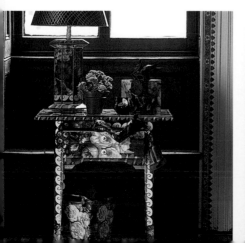

refrigerator, inside and out

Everybody has a refrigerator. Unfortunately, they're usually clunky, occupy immense amounts of space, and are about as interesting as cement blocks. So why not decoupage them—inside and out?

Contact paper is a self-adhesive paper that is widely available in the housewares section of many stores. It's the ultimate self-adhesive paper—there are hundreds of different patterns available, and it's designed to be cleaned easily with soap and water. Contact paper is ideal for the inside of a refrigerator because there is no need to polyurethane the finished work; it's better not to have polyurethane around food anyway, and contact paper is durable. Choose a geometric pattern, a floral design, or a copy of an English tile—anything that suits your fancy.

INTERIOR

1. Empty the refrigerator and turn it off. Remove the shelves and drawers to make things a bit easier on yourself. Also, clean the inside (something you should probably do anyway).

2. Measure the interior of the refrigerator with a tape measure. Break up the work surface into sections, like the back wall, the left side, the door panel, etc. Total the measurements to determine the amount of paper you need.

3. Add ¼″ to all measurements to allow enough paper to make turns and overlaps. (You can trim any excess later.) Use a pencil and yardstick to lay out a piece for each interior surface. Use scissors to cut out the pieces.

4. Remove the release paper from the back of the contact paper, and apply the sticky surface to the interior. To avoid unsightly air pockets, first press only one edge into position; hold the opposite end away from the surface. Then, with your free hand, slowly and evenly smooth the paper into place. If you do wind up with an air pocket, don't despair. Just prick the pocket gently with a razor blade (allowing the air to escape), and then press it out flat. It will not be noticeable once the project is complete.

5. With a single-edge razor blade, trim away excess paper.

6. That's it! Just don't use the new-found attractiveness of your refrigerator interior as an excuse to open it up for yet another slice of pound cake. And now that it's so pretty, keep it clean!

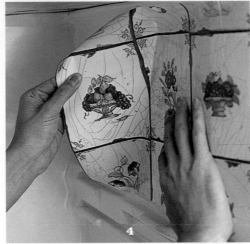

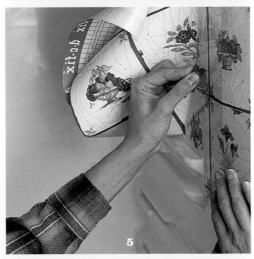

WHAT YOU'LL NEED

REFRIGERATOR

TAPE MEASURE

CONTACT PAPER

PENCIL

SCISSORS

STRAIGHT PIN

SINGLE-EDGE RAZOR BLADE

For my refrigerator, I chose nine panels from Fra Angelico's Life of the Virgin, *then laser-copied them so that I had a lot of repeats to use as "tiles." But you can cover your icebox with Dean Martin and Jerry Lewis, if you want to. I'll never understand why but, hey, it's your icebox.*

One final note here: Maybe I repaired this fridge too many times with too many coats of polyurethane, or perhaps I hurried to get it done and didn't leave enough drying time between coats. Whatever the reason, the polyurethane has somehow developed an antique-looking crackled finish. Everybody thinks I did it on purpose to achieve a special look. I didn't. Why I am I confessing the truth now? My point is to stay calm—just because something goes wrong doesn't mean that you can't live with it or that your friends won't regard it as pure genius. Just keep quiet and let them convince you how brilliant you are.

1. Use a tape measure to measure the area you want to decoupage and make sure you have enough images to cover the surface. You see, those math classes in high school were important after all.

2. Using Grade 220 sandpaper, sand the areas you plan to decoupage. You don't have to sand all that much, just enough to dull the shiny finish and get rid of the dirt.

3. With a 2″ sponge brush, apply a generous amount of PVA adhesive to the back of one image. Carefully press it into position on the refrigerator exterior, smoothing out any creases gently with your fingertips. Clean up excess glue with a water-dampened sponge. Repeat with the remaining images. When you come face-to-face with a door handle or hinge, don't panic. Just score the art with your scissors at the exact point where you've met the obstruction, and then cut away that bit of the image to make it fit perfectly around the handle. Don't worry if you cut away too much; you can always put a small patch over the mistake.

4. Allow the glue to dry overnight.

5. Using a sponge brush, apply at least 2 coats of a semigloss acrylic-based polyurethane to protect your work, letting each coat dry at least 2 hours before applying the next. If you can find the time, 3 or 4 coats would be ideal.

WHAT YOU'LL NEED

TAPE MEASURE

REFRIGERATOR

IMAGES

GRADE 220 SANDPAPER

PVA ADHESIVE

CELLULOSE SPONGE

SCISSORS

SPONGE BRUSH

SEMIGLOSS ACRYLIC-BASED POLYURETHANE

Remember, a refrigerator door is opened a few zillion times in its lifetime, so durability (especially around the handles) is definitely an issue, particularly if you've got a dexterous dog capable of looking after himself. That's why it's smart to produce and save some extra copies of the images. Keep them in an envelope in the drawer closest to your refrigerator. If an area gets damaged, all you have to do is lightly sand the damaged area with Grade 400 sandpaper, then apply the fresh images from your files.

post-it® note cabinet

One of the enduring myths of America is the age-old tension between country and city, between Kansas and Manhattan. Basically, I think the myth is a lot of hooey, dreamt up by Hollywood screenwriters to add dash to their stories. All it's done is create a bunch of Kansans who think New York is a moral wasteland and a bunch of New Yorkers who think Kansas is a wasteland, period. Well, I was born on a farm in Minnesota and was raised in a suburb of Kansas City and I now live in New York, and I love all these places. As a symbol of this trilateral love, I created a spice cabinet that's a melding of country and city, Midwest and East Coast and the 3M corporate headquarters in Minneapolis—all courtesy, of course, of New Decoupage.

The basic "bones" of this cabinet are 100 years old. A friend of mine in Springhill, Kansas, built the shelving using boards he salvaged from an old barn. I made a big mistake and painted it blue. But the more I looked at it, the more the bold color grew on me; it just needed to be toned down. I considered painting on some stripes, or perhaps even a diagonal design. Then I realized: Why paint, when you can paper? And right there on top of my desk I spied perfect little squares—Post-it® notes —that when applied in a diagonal pattern, created a playful decorative pattern on the previously horrid blue. The result is an Italian Renaissance design, via Kansas, Manhattan, and the Post-it® note factory.

1. Prepare the cabinet surface by following the instructions that begin on page 24.

2. With a 2" bristle brush apply wheat paste to the back of one Post-it® note square. Turn the note corner side up, so the square is a diamond. Beginning at the top, in the center of the cabinet, press the square into position. Repeat the process, working down until you finish a single vertical row. Stand back and make sure you've got it straight. Then working toward the sides, fill in the remaining vertical rows until you get to the edges. By starting at the center, the "bleed" on the edges will be the same on left and right; make sure the vertical rows are equally spaced.

3. Use a wet brayer to squeeze out excess paste. (If, by chance, you did find a weathered cabinet like mine with some surface texture that you want to keep, use your fingertips instead of the brayer to gently rub and press the paper into the grain of the wood. The fiber of the paper will meld with the texture of the wood, giving the impression that the squares are actually painted on.) Clean up the excess with a water-dampened sponge. Allow to dry overnight.

4. Using a 2" sponge brush, finish with at least 2 coats of acrylic-based polyurethane, allowing each coat to dry thoroughly. If your spouse never takes you out to dinner and you open these cabinet doors 3 or more times a day, use a brush to apply 2 coats of an oil-based polyurethane. Or consider getting a new spouse.

5. We finished our cabinet with 2 legs robbed from an overstuffed side chair a neighbor tossed out. The chair was pretty ratty, but those legs caught my eye. They were easily attached with vinyl epoxy from the hardware store. If you plan to mount your cabinet on the wall, I guess you don't really need the legs, but stick 'em on anyway if you like the look.

WHAT YOU'LL NEED

PAINTED CABINET

2" BRISTLE BRUSH

WHEAT PASTE

POST-IT® NOTES

BRAYER

CELLULOSE SPONGE

2" SPONGE BRUSH

ACRYLIC-BASED POLYURETHANE

OIL-BASED POLYURETHANE (OPTIONAL)

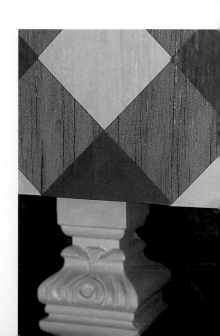

coffee table

AN HOMAGE TO "MARBLE"

The art of faux marble is wonderful. Expert craftsmen spend their lives figuring out how to create with oils and paper the exact image of marble. I have seen examples of it that are so extraordinary that I've had to touch the paint to discover the illusion. I'm impressed, but personally, I can't faux-marble worth a damn. And my reaction to this deficiency is who cares? I can *buy* marbleized paper that is wonderful, and all I have to do is glue it to a table to create a "marble" piece of furniture. Why spend your life figuring out how to marbleize, when you can do something important, like throw a party? All the faux marble you need can be purchased in a paper-goods shop, and it's a lot lighter to carry home than a slab of the real thing.

Take a small table, the kind that sits in front of small sofas. Most people spend pots of money for such a thing only to bury it under cheap romance novels and cheesy magazines, or worse. They use it as a footrest, eat off of it, and generally use it for all manner of things for which it wasn't intended. So, instead of paying a lot, get a used, beat-up table at a flea market (provided you like the shape of it) and decoupage it into something wonderful. The table I started with was secondhand—more like fifteenth-hand, actually—and made of very light wood. I decided to put marbleized paper on it and a half dozen coats of high-gloss polyurethane. Everyone thinks it's marble, until they try to pick it up and discover it's made of cheap wood!

110

1. PREPARE THE SURFACE

Follow the instructions that begin on page 24 to prepare the table's surface.

2. PAINT THE TABLE

Use a brush and a paint primer to prime the table, if necessary. Then use a brush to paint it with the latex enamel paint. As always, you'll probably need at least 2 coats for complete coverage. If you want to, use an artist's brush and gold-leaf paint to highlight any special details on the legs of the table.

3. ADD THE PAPER TOP

You may decide to apply paper across the entire top of the table, or in sections, interspersing it with other images or even using the marbleized paper as a border with other images in the center. I was lucky, my table wasn't all that big, so I was able to do the entire tabletop with just one sheet of faux green marble paper. Hence, no seams. Sheets of faux marble paper can be found as big as 28 × 38″. If you do have to make a seam, put it in the middle of the table. If you tell me you've got to make 2 seams using paper that large, then I think you should consider a smaller, less pretentious coffee table.

It's fairly easy to get large sheets of paper onto a flat surface without air pockets. First, hold the marbleized paper in position over the top of the table. Then, use a hard edge (something like a ruler, or your scissors blade) and score the paper around the perimeter of the tabletop. Just press the hard edge against the paper all along the edge, to leave a crease, enough of one to guide cutting. Use scissors to cut the sheet (or sheets) of paper to the size you need. Relax the paper (see page 51). When relaxing a large sheet of paper or large image, a great thing to have on hand is a plastic window-box liner from the local garden shop. The liner is narrow but

deep enough and wide enough to hold water and the big sheet. First, fill the window-box liner with 3″ or 4″ of warm water. Roll the paper to 2″ to 3″ in diameter. Then immerse it in the water. Once it is saturated, pull on one end of the paper and it will unroll as you raise it out of the water.

4. Using a brush, apply a 50/50 mixture of PVA adhesive and wheat paste onto the tabletop. Lay the relaxed sheet into position. Using a brayer, gently press the paper down flat, wiping up excess water and adhesive with a water-dampened sponge as you work. Allow to dry overnight before trimming the edges by using a straightedge and a new single-edge razor blade.

5. ADD IMAGES (OPTIONAL)

Relax the first image. Use a brush to apply the PVA mixture to the marbleized paper and place the image into position. Use the brayer to press it flat and remove excess glue with the water-dampened sponge. Repeat until all images are in place. Yes, on this table I covered a lot of the marble, but it's a lot better than all the ugly seams I'd have had if I tried to cut and piece the marbleized paper as a border. So, by laying just 3 images on top of just 1 sheet of marbleized paper, I end up with a very complicated (and neat) design. But you don't have to add anything.

6. SEAL THE SURFACE

After allowing the table to dry overnight, use a sponge brush to apply at least 2 coats of acrylic-based polyurethane to the finished paper surface and legs. If you have the patience, build up to at least 5 coats on the top surface of the table; it will give the impression of depth and really protect it. Allow the table to cure for about a week before you use it.

TABLE

PAINT PRIMER

LATEX ENAMEL PAINT

ARTIST'S BRUSH (OPTIONAL)

GOLD-LEAF PAINT (OPTIONAL)

MARBLEIZED PAPER

ADDITIONAL IMAGES

SCISSORS

WINDOW-BOX LINER

50/50 MIXTURE OF PVA/PASTE

BRAYER

CELLULOSE SPONGE

STRAIGHTEDGE

SINGLE-EDGE RAZOR BLADE

SPONGE BRUSH

ACRYLIC-BASED POLYURETHANE

bureau

Who says wallpaper has to be limited to walls? Prepasted wallpaper—not contact paper but real wallpaper, the kind that gets sticky when wet—is one of my favorite papers to use in a variety of ways, especially on painted surfaces. See what wallpaper did for this uninteresting bureau that I inherited from my sister when I left home for college?

This is one of the easiest projects in the book. I used a small bureau, but you could just as easily apply wallpaper to a desk, sideboard, chest, or an étagère. Undistinctive building materials, or a few nicks and lumps in the piece, don't matter because they'll all be covered up. My only suggestion is this: Make a careful examination of the piece to be decoupaged. Look past the surface imperfections, the cheap materials, the poor workmanship —all the things that are wrong with the 20th century. Study the shape *of the piece; make sure that the basic de-*

sign is good. Be critical, because some pieces of furniture are truly hideous and beyond the talents of even the best decoupeur.

If you like the design, look at the walls in the room where your piece of furniture will be placed. If the wallpaper you're applying to the furniture is the same as what's on the wall, be creative when applying it to the furniture. Let's say the pattern on the wallpaper is a long trailing vine with flowers in a 14-inch repeat. Grab your scissors and cut out a part of the design, say, a vine or some flowers. Arrange the cutouts in a pleasing pattern across the surfaces of the bureau. Bunch the vines, cross the vines, use only one vine, or wrap it around the entire piece of furniture. Intersperse the flowers randomly or create a geometric design; use the elements to create something entirely different but equally beautiful.

1. PREPARE AND PAINT THE BUREAU

Follow the instructions that begin on page 24 to clean and prepare the piece. Using a brush, apply 2 coats of paint primer, allowing each coat to dry thoroughly. Paint the bureau with latex enamel paint the same color as the background color on the wallpaper. To get a good match, take a wallpaper sample to a paint store and ask the salesperson to match the color. Don't get frantic if the store hasn't got a computer capable of doing this. Who needs a computer for this? Most of the old-timers in paint stores are still able to match a color by trusting their very experienced eyes. They already know what you need to learn: that the color of the dried paint is a little darker than the color of wet paint in the can. You can easily match the color yourself. Just compare the wallpaper sample with the paint chips in the store's display. Once you find one you want, the salesperson can mix it for you. And anyway, whoever said it has to be *exactly* the same color? *Approximately* the same color always looks good to my eye. Allow the paint to dry overnight.

2. DO SOME PLANNING

If it's a lattice design you are after, measure and pencil in some lines to guide you.

3. CUT THE WALLPAPER

From the wallpaper use scissors to cut out the birds, vines, leaves, or whatever images you plan to use.

4. APPLY THE CUTOUTS

Yes, the wallpaper is prepasted. But, the bureau is going to get some wear and tear. So, adhere it with generous amounts of PVA. Clean up excess glue with a damp sponge.

5. ALLOW THE BUREAU TO DRY OVERNIGHT

Then use a sponge brush to apply two coats of acrylic-based polyurethane and let dry completely.

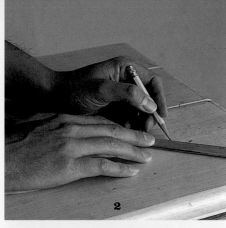

WHAT YOU'LL NEED

LEAD PENCIL

RULER OR STRAIGHTEDGE

BUREAU

PAINT PRIMER

LATEX ENAMEL PAINT

WALLPAPER

SCISSORS

BASIN OF WATER

SYNTHETIC CELLULOSE SPONGE

SPONGE BRUSH

ACRYLIC-BASED POLYURETHANE

PVA ADHESIVE

family dining room table

Amid all the talk about family values over the past few years, it's sobering to recall Sigmund Freud's observation: "Families are the cauldron of all neuroses." A table like this can be very helpful when people say to you, "What's wrong with you? Don't you know how to behave?" Then you can proudly point to your dining room table and respond, "Of course I don't know how to behave. And here are the reasons." You can have vivid color photos of Uncle John, banished from the family for reasons long forgotten. Or old black-and-whites of Aunt Sally before she put on those disputed extra pounds. And of course, what study of family neuroses would be complete without photographs of those two prime forces of family dysfunction, Mom and Dad? On the other hand, you might actually want to create this table because you truly love your family.

1. LAYING THE FOUNDATION

After preparing the surface, choose a faux marble paper that will look good in your dining room and apply it according to the instructions for the coffee table on page 110. By "good" I mean it looks good with both your dining room decor *and* your mother-in-law's chosen hair color.

2. EQUALIZE PHOTO TONES

Great Aunt Elsie's photo has mellowed with age and has a nice sepia tint to it, but the photo of Cousin Becky's latest little bundle of joy looks like something created by the colorists at Nintendo. If you don't like the looks of these 2 photos on the same table, don't panic. There's a solution. Set your color laser copier to Old-fashioned Photo Image. Then copy the photo of Becky's baby. The result will be a baby's photograph that shares not only Aunt Elsie's large earlobes and buck teeth, but also the sepia tones of her photograph. While you are at it, make laser copies of Aunt Elsie's photo and all those you plan to use. Why run the risk of ruining the originals?

3. TELL YOUR FAMILY STORY

Experiment with the arrangement of your chosen images. Juxtapose images for artistic and/or family political reasons. You might put Uncle Bob and Uncle Walt at different ends of the table, owing to the fact that they haven't spoken to each other since the 1971 July 4th picnic. Or you might have a cousins' corner, where all the cousins are together. Set up individual family units within the overall family group. Experiment. Be provocative, be compassionate, be funny, be spiteful. Create alliances where they don't exist. Provide a chronology of family life, starting with your great-grandparents and running up to the latest arrival. This is your opportunity to represent history or to re-create it.

4. APPLY THE IMAGES

Use a bush to apply a 50/50 mixture of PVA adhesive and wallpaper paste onto the first image. Lay the image into position. Use a wet brayer to roll the image flat. With a water-dampened sponge, wipe away excess glue. Apply the rest of the images, remembering to let each one dry thoroughly before applying another on top of it. If you choose, embellish the images after they dry by using a fine-nib gold pen to add decorative designs or short messages.

5. PROTECT YOUR FAMILY

Use a sponge brush to apply at least 2 coats of acrylic-based polyurethane. Allow the table to cure for at least 2 weeks. Use the curing time as an excuse for not inviting your in-laws to dinner.

6. LIVE WITH THE FUTURE

This table should be considered a living project, meaning that, if your family is anything like mine, you are never going to be able to finish it. When your niece Kim has another 9-pounder, you can squeeze in a tiny photo of the tot wherever you think it looks best. Just sand the area lightly with Grade 400 sandpaper. Apply the newest family member and finish the area with acrylic-based polyurethane. This applies also to those kicked out of the family, say, by divorce or imprisonment. You can put a red line through them or simply glue the image of another family member over the one you want to forget.

WHAT YOU'LL NEED

DINING ROOM TABLE

PAINT PRIMER

LATEX ENAMEL PAINT

FAMILY PHOTOS

SCISSORS

50/50 MIXTURE OF PVA/PASTE

BRAYER

CELLULOSE SPONGE

FINE-NIB GOLD PEN (OPTIONAL)

SPONGE BRUSH

ACRYLIC-BASED POLYURETHANE

GRADE 400 SANDPAPER

room
by
room: ARCHITECTURAL ELEMENTS

RIGHT: *All the architectural decoupage elements of this hallway were taken from the same design of wallpaper which leads up the stairs underneath the rail. The birds and florals above it were cut and pasted onto a gold leaf paint and then preserved under acrylic polyurethane. The vines around the doorways came from the same wallpaper. The lattice ceiling was also created from elements within the basic paper.*

Page after page I've been beating the same drum, trying to explain how New Decoupage offers more opportunities for enhancing total interior environments than its gentrified history suggests. This holds true when it comes to decoupaging architectural elements, a process that in turn often creates new architectural elements. This aspect of New Decoupage is especially exciting if you live in a space that is composed of simple, flat surfaces, like the plain interiors that are standard issue in most modern apartment buildings and homes. In these living spaces the walls, ceilings, and doors are plain, the trim is generally unadorned, and architecturally there is little to relieve the wide expanses of space. To make matters worse, these interiors are usually painted in muted shades of gray and white, lending them a sterile air that's more institution than home.

Of course, you will personalize your living space, whether by means of a table of family photos, a desk bought at a flea market, or a pile of clothes you've left in the corner by the bed. But these things are transitory; they change as soon as you rearrange the photos, move the papers on the desk, or do the laundry. To give your space a more permanent personal touch, New Decoupage can be just the ticket.

Having mentioned the sterile similarity that marks so many new dwellings, I feel obliged to say that many of the photographs of architectural decoupage in this book are of projects I created within a gorgeous landmark house (see page 142). You might argue that anything would look good in such a house, and I suppose that's partly true. But my feeling is that New Decoupage is even more dramatic in a simple, modern space. This is because it can transform it into a space with a totally new feeling, as opposed to emphasizing existing and unique architectural elements, as we have done here.

When creating architectural elements through decoupage, I have a strong preference for using wallpaper. In the first place, most wallpaper patterns are fairly large designs, big enough to work nicely in a big space. Second, today many wallpapers are available prepasted, which makes them easy to work with. Third, and this is very important, wallpaper is good-quality paper; it's very easy to cut, not too flimsy, not too thick. We all know cutting is important in decoupage, and that is especially true in architectural decoupage. When I talk about using wallpaper in this context, I'm not talking about simply gluing roll after roll to a wall or ceiling, although that's O.K. I'm talking about cutting out figures and patterns from the paper and creating architectural scenes with them.

For example, for the entrance hallway shown here, I selected a

beautiful Schumacher wallpaper with a 21-inch repeat and very intricate designs (geometrics, botanicals, birds). I cut up the pattern four ways from Sunday and then rearranged the pieces in a myriad of different spaces, creating my own interesting and attractive designs. Since the color palette is from the same roll of paper, there is a sense of unity in the different arrangements that makes the whole project work. And it was surprisingly easy to do.

RIGHT: *Flowers can adorn your mantel year round if they're pasted to the wall, keeping company with favorite books and other assorted images.*

Wall Scenes

You can, of course, simply wallpaper a room from floor to ceiling. That's a great idea if the walls are in bad shape; wallpaper can hide a multitude of sins. But what I'm talking about here is using elements of the wallpaper to create whimsical borders. Not only does such a design look interesting, it can be very economical. Suppose you've found one of the world's great wallpapers that costs $150 or more per roll. Buy just one roll, cut it up, and apply its elements to different parts of the wall, painted to match. Choose a color from the palette of

colors in the wallpaper, and don't always look for the obvious. The most pleasing choice might be a subtle color from the many colors in the wallpaper. How much paint do you need? Measure the space, and let whoever's behind the paint counter tell you how much you'll need. Then paint the walls that color, following the manufacturer's instructions. Allow the paint to dry overnight, then begin your decorating.

The easiest method is to cut figures from prepasted wallpaper; then all you have to do is wet the paper and apply them to the wall. However, don't be limited by this easy way out; if your intention is to re-create a scene from the Battle of Waterloo, chances are you won't find the images you want on a piece of wallpaper, at least not all of them. So use the whole arsenal of your collected library. Laser-copy images, if necessary. Enlarge them to the desired scale. Think really big. I know someone who re-created on his basement wall the interior of the old Polo Grounds at 4:05 P.M. on October 3, 1951, the exact moment that Bobby Thomson hit his famous home run.

All right, I made that up. But if you've got some time on your hands and Bobby Thomson is somebody you really care about, get going, you can do it!

Arrange the images starting first by taping them gently around the frame of a door or window. Try garlands draped out from the top, in the center. Try two birds darting at the corners. Create sylvan scenes; create riotous scenes. Create, create, create. And keep at it until you've created a scene that pleases you. After all, you've got to live there. When you have an arrangement you like, it's time to get serious. If you are using prepasted wallpaper, all you have to do is dip the pieces into a basin of water and press them into position with a damp sponge. Then use the sponge to wipe away any excess water. If it's not prepasted, brush some wallpaper paste onto the wall, position the cutouts, press them down with the damp sponge, and wipe away excess paste.

Some wallpapers do not have an accompanying border paper. The Schumacher paper I wanted to use did not have one, so I created one from the existing paper. I isolated a single design, a 4-inch width of a stripe. This was simply pasted to the outline of the door, and I mitered the corners at the top.

MANIPULATE THOSE IMAGES!

When creating a free-flowing design, it's sometimes necessary to manipulate the images a little to get the look right. If your cutouts are all vertical, such as flowers that are only a few inches wide but nearly a foot high, they'll look lovely going up the sides of the door. Use the same flowers on the lintel, however, and all people will be able to think of is a crewcut grown out of control. To avoid this, either trim back the flowers to 3 to 4 inches when they cross the lintel, or angle them slightly so that they face down. If you are using animals—for instance, birds—trim them a bit, or position them horizontally to reduce the height of the crossing design. Stand back and look at the total effect. That is what your visitors are going to see, not the two birds at the very top who are missing their tail feathers.

119

ceiling moldings

Beware of interior designers who are in a rush to decorate moldings. White on this part, red on that part, gold leaf on another. It gets even crazier when people begin to marbleize their moldings. All that work, and all that money! Forget polychroming with paint and gold leaf. Forget faux-marbleizing with paint. If you're lucky enough to have moldings and you want them to look opulent, why not paper them? The use of marbleized paper is nothing short of stunning. Plus, because the molding is up a good 8 feet or more, snoopy friends won't spot any little mistakes while they are wondering from whence came your prodigious marbleizing talents.

1. Be a good scout and remember to properly prepare your surface; everything you need to know to do that you'll find in the instructions that begin on page 24.

the ends of each strip of paper. This may be unsightly when you are looking at it from the top of the ladder, but the seam isn't noticeable when you get down on the floor.

WHAT YOU'LL NEED

SCISSORS
FAUX MARBLE PAPER
1″ BRISTLE BRUSH
WALLPAPER PASTE
CELLULOSE SPONGE
STRAIGHTEDGE
SINGLE-EDGE RAZOR BLADES

2. With scissors cut strips of the marbleized paper ¼″ wider than the moldings. Using a brush, apply wallpaper paste to the back of one strip.

3. Put the strip into place, smoothing it onto the molding with a water-dampened sponge. It's okay to overlap

4. Trim the edges by using a straightedge and a single-edge razor blades. Use a fresh blade for each strip of paper because you are cutting through damp paper, into paint and possibly wood or plaster. This causes the blades to get dull very quickly, and a dull blade is going to tear the paper instead of cutting it smoothly.

kitchen cabinets

SECTIONALIZE A LARGE IMAGE

Problem: The largest piece of paper the copier will print is 11 × 17 inches, and your image needs to be larger. Solution: Let the machine reproduce the image one section at a time. Then all you have to do is match them up. If you still don't understand this and won't go to the therapist to find out why, just take the image and cabinet measurements to the copy shop. Tell the salesperson what you want and watch what comes out of the machine.

I had the perfect image to apply to my kitchen cabinets, a painting of a beautiful earthenware vase of flowers that just seemed to belong in the room. Only one problem: The original image measured 10 by 16 inches, and I needed it big, real big, to cover some uninspired built-in kitchen cabinets. Using a laser copier, I was able to create the exact number and size of images that I needed (see page 42). The result are cabinets that are beautiful as well as functional.

Now everybody, including my editor, looks at these cabinets and says to me, "I won't ever be able to do that." Well, maybe my editor can't, but you can. Really. If you're still scared, you can pay me a ton of money to come do it for you.

1. PREPARE THE SURFACE

Remove the cabinet handles. Follow the instructions that begin on page 24 to clean and prepare the surface. Use a brush to apply 2 coats of paint primer, allowing each coat to dry thoroughly.

2. MEASURE

Use a tape measure to measure each space you want to cover. I decided to put my image in 5 spaces. So I measured the width and height of each space and wrote the measurements down.

3. EXPLORE MULTIPAGE ENLARGING

Take the original image to a copy shop and learn how to use the multipage enlarging function. After adjusting the colors and telling the machine the size you want the copies to be, the machine will print the enlarged copy onto several separate sheets of paper (see the photo). Think of the sheets as pieces in a very simple jigsaw puzzle. It's always a good idea to have the machine produce 2 sets of copies at a time —don't try to cut corners costwise here— because if you make a mistake and have to make copies of the same image a few days later, you may not be able to match the colors exactly. (In fact, it's a good idea to make extra copies for *any* project.)

4. ASSEMBLE THE PUZZLE

Lay out the images in the correct positions and use scissors to trim away the excess, or white borders.

5. RELAX THE PAPER

Immerse a section, one at a time, in the kitchen sink filled with warm water.

6. APPLY THE ADHESIVE

Use a 2″ bristle brush to apply a 50/50 mixture of PVA adhesive and wheat paste onto the entire front of one cabinet door.

7. APPLY THE FIRST IMAGE

Remove the image from the water and place it into position, smoothing it flat with a brayer.

8. GET READY FOR THE SECOND IMAGE

Immerse the next section of the image. While it is in the water, add a little of the PVA–wheat paste mixture onto the previous image where the second image will overlap.

9. APPLY THE SECOND IMAGE

Remove the second image from the water and apply it as you did the first image.

10. KEEP IT CLEAN

As you work, clean up excess water and adhesive with a water-dampened sponge.

11. COMPLETE THE PUZZLE

Repeat the process with all the images until the picture is complete.

12. SEAL THE SURFACE

After you've allowed the creation to dry overnight, touch up any blemishes or white edges with colored pencils. Then, using a sponge brush, apply 3 coats of acrylic-based polyurethane to protect it, allowing each coat to dry thoroughly.

13. ACCESS YOUR CHEERIOS

Replace the cabinet handles.

14. REWARD YOURSELF FOR A JOB WELL DONE

Give yourself a huge pat on the back. Everyone else on your block spent the day watching the soaps.

WHAT YOU'LL NEED

2″ BRISTLE BRUSH

PAINT PRIMER

TAPE MEASURE

IMAGE

SCISSORS

50/50 MIXTURE OF PVA/PASTE

BRAYER

CELLULOSE SPONGE

COLORED PENCILS

1″ SPONGE BRUSH

ACRYLIC-BASED POLYURETHANE

GRADE 400 SANDPAPER

PAPER TILES

A great decoupeur doesn't always use a recognizable image. You can and should use patterns that you create on your own. These kitchen cabinets were decoupaged with construction and handmade papers.

Sure, they aren't going to last the way ceramic tiles would. They are going to get some wear and tear, but who says I have to live with this design forever? In fact, I can replace a paper tile in about 2 minutes for less than a nickel. That's no small benefit. Try replacing one of those 1920s peach-colored tiles in your master bathroom, the one your nephew Brandon took a hammer to, if you want to really appreciate the value of paper tiles.

The ink in construction papers often bleeds when it gets wet, so forgo relaxing the paper before adhering it to your surface. Use a 50/50 PVA/paste mix and brush it onto the back of each tile with a 1-inch sponge brush, then use a dry brayer to flatten it into place. It's that easy.

baseboards

EXPRESS YOURSELF THROUGH REPETITION

Don't feel obliged to use traditional architectural designs. True, trefoils and
quatrefoils are designed to be applied to architectural details such as baseboards, but you can use almost any image. The repeated element can be
a small sailing ship, or a baseball, or a majolica pot filled with dried flowers;
the image itself is almost secondary to the effect it creates.

Everybody has some kind of base-board, and New Decoupage can liven them up. By applying, in a repeating series, a number of small elements—such as a quatre-foil or fleur-de-lis—you provide an unexpected decorative anchor that not only engages the eye but enhances your reputation as a thorough eccentric. If your base-board is too small for this kind of treatment, and most contempo-rary baseboards I've looked at are too small, create the illusion of a larger board by painting or pa-pering one. Some wallpaper bor-ders look great at the base of a room rather than up around the ceiling. Or you might measure up a foot, run a strip of masking tape around the room at that level, and paint yourself a baseboard in a contrasting color.

Measure the length of the base-board and determine at what in-tervals you want the chosen design to appear. Then calculate how many copies of that image you'll need. Cut out each image and adhere it to the baseboard with wallpaper paste, removing any excess paste with a water-dampened sponge.

Note: When copying the same im-age a few hundred times, it's a good idea to fill out an 11×17 page with as many originals of the image as possible. Then, by pressing the copy button once, you get, say, eight images or maybe more. Ganging the images like this saves time and money, which you can donate to a good charity.

chef's cabinet

Congratulations! You've arrived at the last project in the book and you probably think you know all there is to know about New Decoupage. And while that's pretty close to the truth, you're never too smart to learn something more.

Cutting and adhering shelf paper is, I suppose, decoupage at its most minimalistic. However, as with most things minimal, I think we can do better. So if you're planning to decorate the inside of your cabinets, consider something more inspired than a pretty shelf paper. If you're wondering what to cook for dinner, who better to tell you than Julia Child, Jacques Pepin, James Beard, Edna Lewis, Simone Beck, Pierre Franey, Escoffier, or your mother? Why not line the inside of your cabinet walls with enlarged copies of their photographs? Just remember to give me credit when you get offered a job in the kitchen at the Tour d'Argent. (Lots of complimentary dinners would be fine.)

1. After you've chosen and enlarged your favorite chefs you are ready to apply them to the inside of your cabinets (see pages 24 and 42 on proper surface preparation and enlarging images). But wait, Julia's portrait is in color and the rest are black and white? Just use the black and white photo option on the laser copier and you can get Julia to match the rest. And don't be so cheap and sneaky and try to do this on your black and white office copier. Always use a laser copier for all of your photo images. You'll get better resolution every time, even with black and white photos.

2. If you can't find a brush, just use a damp sponge to spread your adhesive evenly over the area that Jacques Pepin is going to cover. You see, the rules of New Decoupage really are flexible. A PVA/wallpaper paste mix would be ideal here, however, if you're out of wallpaper paste and out of cash and have really read all of this book then you are probably accomplished enough by now to use straight PVA. You decide what to do.

3. Relax the image in your kitchen sink, which naturally you have filled with warm water. Now place the image into position and use your brayer to press it flat.

4. I like this big sponge to clean up the excess water and glue. A couple of light strokes over Jacques and the job is done.

5. I cut the border/frames freehand from this wrapping paper. Remember the pot on the shelf? And the framed decoupage apples in the back? Scenes always look better, I think, if they share some common design elements; what do you think?

6. Having cut out the strips for the border and the frames, hold them up around your chefs who have been allowed to dry thoroughly (probably 2 to 4 hours). Still think your chosen paper is the right choice? Maybe it would look better pointing down? Don't ask your kids; make up your own mind. But the point, really, is to keep on thinking. Now that you have unlocked some of your own creative potential, you never know what ideas might materialize. Next, extend the strips to the lengths you need and cut them to the correct size with your scissors.

7. Use your tried-and-true gluing skills to get them cleanly into place. Allow it all to dry overnight and then protect it from your kids with two or three coats of acrylic polyurethane.

8. Now go plan a four star dinner for your spouse. Send the kids over to the grandparents' house. Every book, even a crafts book, should have a happy ending.

WHAT YOU'LL NEED

CHEF PHOTOS

CELLULOSE SPONGE

50/50 PVA/WHEAT PASTE MIX

BRAYER

WRAPPING PAPER

SCISSORS

1″ SPONGE BRUSH

ACRYLIC-BASED POLYURETHANE

epilogue

TOP RIGHT: *Here's a nutty idea, actually a fruity idea. Cut up some oranges and bananas, put them in the oven between two cookie sheets at the lowest temperature until they're dry, about 12 hours for oranges and 6 for bananas. Stick them onto a lampshade with a glue gun. Do not eat.*

"To boldly go where no man has gone before" is not only the world's most famous split infinitive but also a good description of where New Decoupage is heading in the next century.

The future of decoupage naturally depends on the decoupers who will be practicing it. And now that they've been released from the creative confines of the old decoupage past, there's just no end to the creative possibilities available. Using materials from themundane to the magnificient and with cutting tools as technologically advanced as the personal computer or as down to earth as a sharp kitchen knife, the new age New Decoupeur might just surprise and delight you with a whole smorgasbord of new ideas.

What decoupeurs have done for the past four hundred years with scissors and glue will, in the future, be done some with personal computers. Think Monty Python. Remember those collages that depicted immense badgers, total frontal nudity, hot-air balloons, Victorian industrialists with black mustaches, and an assortment of English icons? When the Pythons were putting together those collages to tuck in between the hilarious comic skits, they did so with X-acto knives, scissors, and glue. Then they manipulated the images to suggest movement. It was one of the earliest examples of decoupage going high tech, at least in the sense that the images wound up as a part of the videotapes that became "Monty Python's Flying Circus." Today, all that work would be done digitally. Instead of creating with scissors, paper, and glue, the avant-garde decoupeur can create with no more than a mouse, a computer, a scanner, and the right software (such as Adobe PhotoShop or other widely available image-processing applications).

It's pretty simple. Find an image you like and scan

ABOVE: *If you've got a computer, scanner, and the proper software, you can cut and paste your brother's eyes and forehead onto body parts of Mick Jagger, Dolly Parton, Evander Holyfield, and Edith Bunker. No, it's not the same as cross dressing.*

LEFT: *Don't throw out any scrap or bit of paper. Save it all and cut it into tiny bits that you sort by color, pattern, and texture. Then compose it microscopically, bit by bit, with tweezers until you've "painted" a scene. You'll be amazed at what you create.*

the image into the computer. You just feed it through, and the computer reads it and stores it. Then, with a flick of the mouse, you can call up the image on the computer screen. From there you can do what you want with it. Distort it, isolate elements within it, steal from it, add to it. You just need your 10-year-old nephew to explain how it all works.

For those of us who resist modern technologies like computers, microwaves, and egg substitutes, there remains a New Decoupage for the new age. We need only expand our concept of what we are going to isolate (cut) and how we are going to combine (adhere) it. For instance, you might find wonderful designs on the fruit in your fridge. Or discover something special on a 1940s dress that's been crammed in the back of a closet. Consider creative uses for things like sewing patterns, dollar bills, dice, dominoes, marbles, colorful wooden balls, glitter, and if one of your adhesives

TOP: *Here's a sophisticated variation on a shade: add some antique buttons, hat pins, anything pretty.*

ABOVE: *Here's something you can do with that out of date sewing pattern—turn it into a lampshade. Cut and shape it to size, then attach it to a translucent shade with a glue gun.*

RIGHT: *Express yourself in 3-dimensional decoupage. Hold the composition of your life together with refrigerator magnets, rubber bands, push pins, and tape.*

LEFT: *Anybody who has a really great photograph like this one that's still in a drawer needs to start at the beginning and reread this book. For the rest of us deciding how to decorate the frame consider this. . . if brightly colored balls look great, then use brightly colored balls.*

BELOW: *Make your home happier and healthier with this orange peel decor. Eat the oranges, gold leaf the balls, and paste on the peelings in countless patterns both traditional and abstract.*

doesn't bind them together try using rubber bands, wire, staple guns, or magnets. Or maybe you're indecisive and even unable to make a binding commitment as transitory as a refrigerator magnet, so why not really indulge in all your neurosis and turn your home into a living three-dimensional decoupage museum. Arrange things, rearrange things, change your mind, make up your mind, don't make up your mind, amuse yourself, frighten your family and friends. No one is going to commit you for having a bit of fun. So go ahead and open up your own new and very personal page of decoupage history.

RIGHT: *One absolutely essential component of New Decoupage is always going to be your new idea. So what do you do if you haven't got a lampshade for your newly decoupaged lamps? Try not to lose any sleep over it. Just toss out the old shades, turn out the lamps, and you'll soon dream up something new.*

OPPOSITE: *If your cabinets lack architectural detail, New Decoupage allows you to create it. Fake a fresco from the Renaissance and tape some black paper stars onto the sides. If anybody asks you to explain it, just say it makes you happy.* ABOVE: *3-dimensional decoupage is a good excuse to celebrate holidays year round. And what's wrong with that?* FOLLOWING PAGES, LEFT: *Cover some interesting chairs with handmade paper, put them atop your dining room table, and serve off them. You call that crazy? Look, if your guests are still accepting your party invitations, you must be doing something right.* RIGHT: *Instead of handing all your bucks over to casinos, cut up a couple and create some decorative objets for your coffee table. Expand on the casino theme with some coasters made from dice and serve your guests tea from a glitter-covered teapot. Now if that doesn't give them and you a kick, I give up.*

about
the
house

Many of the interiors shown in *New Decoupage* are set in one of New York's most historic and architecturally distinguished buildings: the rectory of St. Paul's Memorial Church (Episcopal) overlooking the harbor of New York, on Staten Island.

Listed in the National Register of Historic Places, this Victorian Gothic Revival structure is also a designated landmark of both the city and state of New York. The architect is one of America's most distinguished 19th-century designers, Edward Tuckerman Potter, whose most well-known buildings are both in Hartford, CT: the Mark Twain House and the Colt Memorial Church. Although Potter designed a number of buildings in New York City, his only remaining edifices are St. Paul's Memorial Church, its rectory, and the impressive Chantry of Grace Church on lower Broadway.

St. Paul's Memorial Church was a gift to the Staten Island parish of Judge Albert Ward, of the wealthy Ward steamship-line family; the church was built as a memorial to his sister. The rectory was erected in 1866 by the parish, and its design was based on an English gatekeeper's lodge.

resources: THE LAST WORD ON DECOUPAGE

My final word of advice for all aspiring Decoupeurs is this… don't spend too much time on this page. It's always tempting to think that the perfect source for whatever you think you need is just a phone call away. But the truth is, almost everything you need to be a wonderful decoupeur is already in your possession: scissors, glue, images, your creative genius, and this book! And if you've read it you know that you can get more of what you need at your local craft, art supply, stationary, or hardware stores, not to mention flea markets and bookstores. Who needs a resource section—unless you got addicted to the wallpaper design you saw on page 29 and simply have to find out where we got it. So, in the spirit of keeping you happy, here's our list.

Ballard Designs
1670 Defoor Avenue NW
Atlanta, GA 30318
(800) 367-2775
(Mirror, p. 12)

**Bentley Brothers/
Crown Decorative Products**
2709 South Park Road
Louisville, KY 40219
(800) 824-4777
(Anaglypta papers, pp. 95, 100, and 143)

Patrick Cunningham
201 East 12th Street, #410
New York, NY 10003
(212) 251-7196
pcunningham@mezzbwn.com
(Photoshop artwork, p. 135)

John Derian Company, Inc.
6 East 2nd Street
New York, NY 10003
(212) 677-3917
(Umbrella stand, p. 129; and candleshades, p. 64)

Donghia, Inc.
485 Broadway
New York, NY 10013
(212) 925-2777
(Gold leaf paper, pp. 122-123)

Durwin Rice Designs
P. O. Box 4253
Blue Springs, MO 64014
(800) 304-8766
durwinrice@aol.com
www.durwinrice.com

Sarah Feather
Redwalls, Burley, Woodhead, Tikley
W. Yorkshire
LS29 7AS Great Britain
011 44 943 864 500
(Lampshade, p. 136)

**Ann and Willy Francois
Willan F.**
R. D. 6, Box 6407
Fast Stroudsburg, PA 18301
(717) 588-9793
(Bookends, p. 23; fruit tray, p. 65; china cabinet, p. 98; and table and accessories, p. 103)

Susan and Wil Johnson
76 Granville Lane
North Andover, MA 01845
(800) 998-3691
collage@mediaone.net
(Chair artwork, p. 135)

**Katzenbach and Warren/
Imperial Wallcoverings**
23645 Mercantile Road
Cleveland, OH 44122
(216) 464-3700
(Wallpapers, pp. 95 (hatboxes), 102, 121, 123, 130, and 142)

N.M.C. Focal Point
P. O. Box 933327
Atlanta, GA 30377
(404) 351-0820
(Ceiling medallions, pp. 101 and 103)

Victor Nelson
128 West 82nd Street
New York, NY 10024
(212) 580-7672
artny@aol.com
(Refrigerator, frame, sunflower bowl with oranges, pp. 136-137; dice and teapot, p. 140; and ornaments, p. 137)

F. Schumacher & Company
79 Madison Avenue
New York, NY 10016
(212) 213-7900
(Wallpapers, pp. 23, 117, 120, 122, 129, and 131)

Katherine Simpson
1793 Twelfth Street
Oakland, CA 94607
(510) 832-7205
(Sewing pattern shade, p. 136)

index